Origami
on the Go!

Origami
on the Go!

MARGARET VAN SICKLEN

WORKMAN PUBLISHING • NEW YORK

Acknowledgments

I never travel solo. My adventures are shared with family and friends, old and new. Thanks to my super talented origami friends who generously contributed their models to this book—Ros Joyce, Rachel Katz, Marc Kirshenbaum, John Montroll, Nick Robinson, Laura Kruskal, and Anita Barbour. Thanks to my editor, Raquel Jaramillo, and her fabulous assistant, Natalie Rinn, whose shared love of travel and paper folding made this book such fun. And many thanks to Susan Bolotin for supporting this project and believing that kids, travel, and origami go together.

Driving north, flying south, sailing east, or cruising west is always an adventure with my turtle dove, Sven Nebelung, by my side. Thanks for always being there.

Library of Congress Cataloging-in-Publication Data is available.

ISBN 978-0-7611-5105-0

Workman books are available at special discounts when purchased in bulk for premiums and sales promotions as well as for fund-raising or educational use. Special editions or book excerpts also can be created to specification. For details, contact the Special Sales Director at the address below.

Design by Lisa Hollander with Nancy Mace

Workman Publishing Company, Inc.
225 Varick Street
New York, NY 10014-4381
www.workman.com

Printed in Malaysia
First printing June 2009

10 9 8 7 6 5 4 3 2

Credits

Front cover: Photo insets clockwise from top left: Colin Anderson/Getty Images; Maple Tree Art/Shutterstock; Jacques Alexandre/age fotostock; Illustration: Art Glazer (bottom second from left)

Back cover: Photo insets clockwise from top left: Marek Patzer/age fotostock; Neo Edmund/Shutterstock; Mark Yarchoan/Shutterstock

Interior: **age fotostock** Jacques Alexandre p.133 (top photo inset); Gonzalo Azumendi p. 7 (top center); Bill Bachmann p. 7 (bottom center); Rodolfo Benítez p. 36; Juniors Bildarchiv p. 96 (bottom right nightingale); Alexander Kupka p. 7 (top right); Kupka p. 51 (bottom right); Michael S. Nolan p. 73 (bottom right); Marek Patzer p. 113 (top illustration inset); Thomas Ruhl p. 83 (swordfish); Achim Sass p. 40; Hans Strand p. 63 (top left photo inset); SuperStock p. 6 (top left and bottom right); The Print Collector p. 37 (map and inset map); Travel Pix Collection p. 7 (top left); Vidler p. 6 (bottom left); **Getty Images** Colin Anderson p. 127 (top left photo inset); Robert Daly p. 2 (bottom right); David Deas p. xi (bottom right), p. 120 (bottom left); GK Hart/Vikki Hart p. 66 (bottom left); Frans Lemmens p.108 (bottom right koala); Debra McClinton p. 140 (top left); **The Library of Congress Print and Photographs** p. 14 (bottom two right photo insets), 66 (bottom right), 73 (bottom left); **Sam Maslow** p. 80 (top); **National Atlas** p. 76 (bottom inset map).
All origami photographs by Jenna Bascom, Luke Bumgarner and Jen Browning.

To my sister, Sarah, who is always
up for another trip, no matter how
harebrained the plan may be.
And to my young friend,
Shelby Crisp, whose eyes sparkle
with curiosity every time she puts
on her traveling shoes.

Contents

Stunt Plane, page 14

Lucky 7 Plane, page 21

Jumping Frog Business Card, page 44

Pig Finger Puppet, page 37

Raccoon Finger Puppet, page 33

PART TWO

Hoofed, Horned, or Hairy, We Love Them All

Grand Canyon Rattlesnake, page 76

Agra Peacock, page 111

Japanese Samurai Helmet, page 127

PART THREE

Cultural Treasures

PART FOUR

The Voyage Home

PART ONE

Are You Ready for Adventure?

Are you ready? Are you ready to explore a new road, and sleep in a different bed? Are you ready to eat different food . . . even if it's creepy? If your answers are Yes, Yes, and Yes, then let's go!

Origami on the Go! is the perfect traveling companion, whether you're taking a trip around the world or going on a short visit across town. Adventure can begin anywhere at any time—in the backseat of the car, on a cruise ship, or on a plane winging your way to exotic Istanbul. Remember, the trip begins with your first step out your door. So get your origami out, fasten your seatbelts, and enjoy the ride!

Enjoy the Ride

Pack, pack, pack. Rush, rush, rush. Now wait, wait, wait. When are we going to get there? When will the fun begin? Well, wait no longer: Traveling can be the best part of the trip! You don't have to wait until you get there to start having fun. So find a comfortable spot, turn the page, and let *Origami on the Go!* entertain you. Start by mastering the basic steps of origami. Follow the diagrams. Learn to understand the different symbols, arrows, and lines. Once you've mastered the language of paper folding , you'll never get lost on an origami adventure.

Helpful Hints

1. Fold on a flat surface.

2. Review all the diagrams before folding a model.

3. Check the next step as you are folding to see where you're heading.

4. Take it easy and have fun folding! Origami is a brainteaser. Very few people "get it" on the first try. Like any skill, folding will come to you when the moves become automatic.

The 3-Time Charm

There's an old saying that seems like it was invented expressly for origami: "The third time's the charm." See, with origami practice really does make perfect. The first time you fold a model, well, it might not look as great as the picture in the book. That would make sense because you're just trying to figure out the instructions and feel your way through the project. The second time you try, you'll see it looks a whole lot better. But the third time you fold it, I can almost guarantee you: You'll have mastered it!

Just remember: Some projects are easier than others. Go slow, take it easy, and give it three tries.

The inside and outside reverse folds are two common folds.

inside reverse fold

1 Fold and unfold.

2 Slightly open model and fold flap to the inside.

Wow, a wonderful bird's head!

outside reverse fold

A super cute tail!

1 Fold and unfold.

2 Slightly open flap and fold to the outside of the model.

The opposite of inside reverse fold.

Origami Symbols

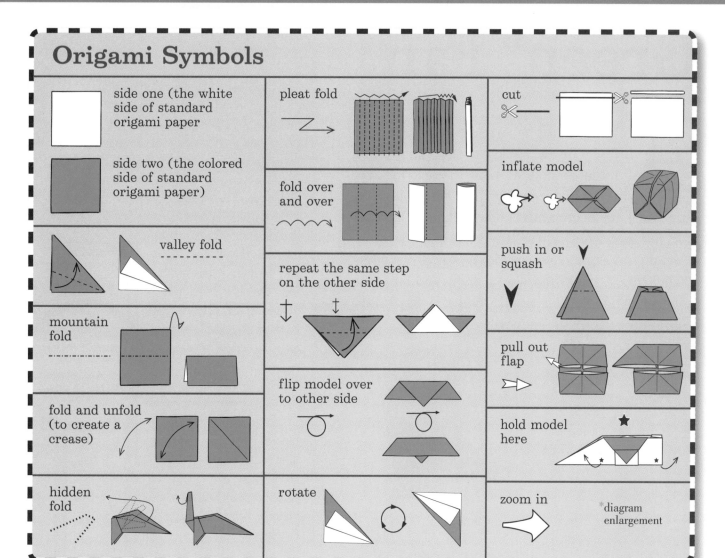

side one (the white side of standard origami paper

side two (the colored side of standard origami paper)

valley fold

mountain fold

fold and unfold (to create a crease)

hidden fold

pleat fold

fold over and over

repeat the same step on the other side

flip model over to other side

rotate

cut

inflate model

push in or squash

pull out flap

hold model here

zoom in

*diagram enlargement

"Green" Fan

Are you aboard an airplane waiting to take off? Or in the backseat of a car waiting for the air-conditioning to kick in? Has the captain (or your folks) just informed you there will be a departure delay? It sure can get hot, hot, hot when you're traveling. Luckily for an Origami traveler like you, a cool breeze is just a few folds away. A paper fan works great—no batteries needed. Wrist getting tired? Pass the fan off to your fellow travelers. They will welcome it.

In 1714, Daniel Gabriel Fahrenheit, a German physicist, invented the mercury thermometer that is still in use today. He introduced the Fahrenheit scale ten years later.

FAHRENHEIT

CELSIUS

In 1742, Anders Celsius, a Swedish astronomer, invented the Celsius scale that is used by almost every country in the world—except the U.S.A.!

WHAT'S HOT & WHAT'S NOT

Next time you're on a plane and the captain reports the local temperature, listen carefully. Is it in Fahrenheit or Celsius? If you live in the United States, you're already familiar with temperatures measured in degrees Fahrenheit. If you're traveling outside the United States, though, you'll hear the weather reports in Celsius. In the Celsius temperature scale, water freezes at 0 degrees and boils at 100 degrees. Pretty logical and very easy to remember. In the Fahrenheit scale, water freezes at 32 degrees and boils at 212 degrees. Not quite so logical or easy to remember. Here's an easy method to use to convert:

So now if the captain reports a local temperature of 28 degrees Celsius, you'll know not to put on your hat and gloves, since that's a balmy 82 degrees Fahrenheit.

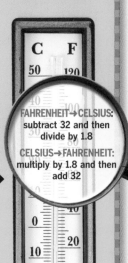

C F
50 190

FAHRENHEIT→CELSIUS:
subtract 32 and then divide by 1.8
CELSIUS→FAHRENHEIT:
multiply by 1.8 and then add 32

How to Fold

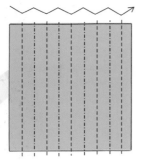

1

Begin with the paper's color side facing up. Pleat fold, back and forth.

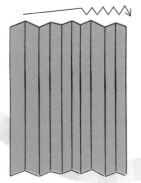

2

The project will look like an accordion or pleated skirt.

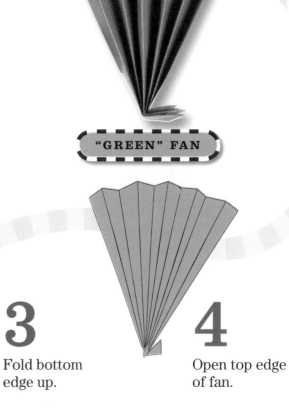

"GREEN" FAN

3

Fold bottom edge up.

4

Open top edge of fan.

"Cheers!" Paper Cup

Has the excitement of traveling got you a bit parched? Is it time to wet your whistle? Where, oh where, is a water fountain when you need one? If you and your traveling companions have just one water bottle to share among you, why not fold a paper cup? In just five folds—presto—you'll have the perfect water cup. Make one for every member of your traveling party and you can all raise your cups together. Three cheers! You're on the road to adventure.

Cheers!

Skål!

Choc-tee!

Santé!

**CHEERS HEARD
'ROUND THE WORLD**

Raise your cup and wish the best to your fellow travelers. Here's to a wonderful trip, good times together, and good times to remember!

CHINA

Yung Sing!

SPAIN

¡Salud!

GERMANY

Prost!

RUSSIA

Na zdorovye!

ITALY

Cin Cin!

ISRAEL

L'chaim!

How to Fold

1 Begin with the paper's white side facing up. Fold in half, bottom to top.

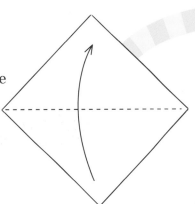

2 Fold top layer down.

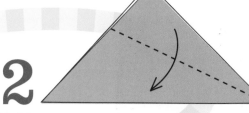

3 Unfold.

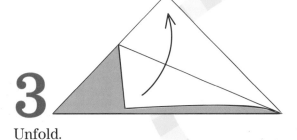

4 Fold right tip to end of crease.

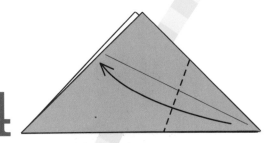

5

Fold left tip to right corner.

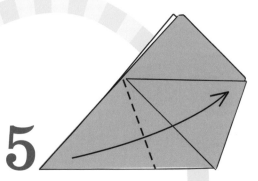

6

Fold top layer down and back layer to back.

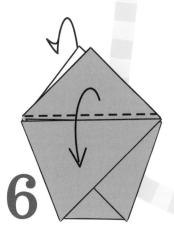

WE ARE HAPPY TO SERVE YOU

"CHEERS!" PAPER CUP

Souvenir Travel Wallet

Want to make a cool souvenir that's also a practical traveling accessory? Purchase a local newspaper on the first day, even if you don't know the language. Choose a section of the paper that has photographs and articles for a little local flavor, and use it to fold a handy travel wallet. Even if you don't have much cash, this jazzy little wallet is a great place to stash the doodads you pick up during your travels.

BYE BYE TOLAR, HELLO EURO

In 2007, Slovenia became the thirteenth European country to replace its national currency with the official currency of the European Union: the euro. Using one currency across most of Europe has simplified the buying and selling of goods and services for international businesses and travelers alike. While I miss the amazing designs and colors of the Dutch guilder and those tiny 1,000 lira notes from Italy, I have to admit it's a lot easier to calculate prices using one currency. Whether I'm negotiating a good deal on a fabulous porcelain pooch in the flea markets of Paris or buying myself a pair of sandals in Athens's Plaka Square, converting euros to dollars is a snap. Phew! I love the euro.

—MVS

CONVERTING EUROS TO DOLLARS:
Number of euros × euro to dollar exchange rate = number of dollars

EXAMPLE: A souvenir costs 30 euros. You want to figure out the equivalent number of U.S. dollars. 30 euro × 1.5 (sample exchange rate) = $45

Austria = Schilling
Belgium = Franc
Finland = Markka
France = Franc
Germany = Deutschmark
Greece = Drachma
Ireland = Punt
Italy = Lira
Luxembourg = Franc
Netherlands = Guilder
Portugal = Escudo
Slovenia = Tolar
Spain = Peseta

How to Fold

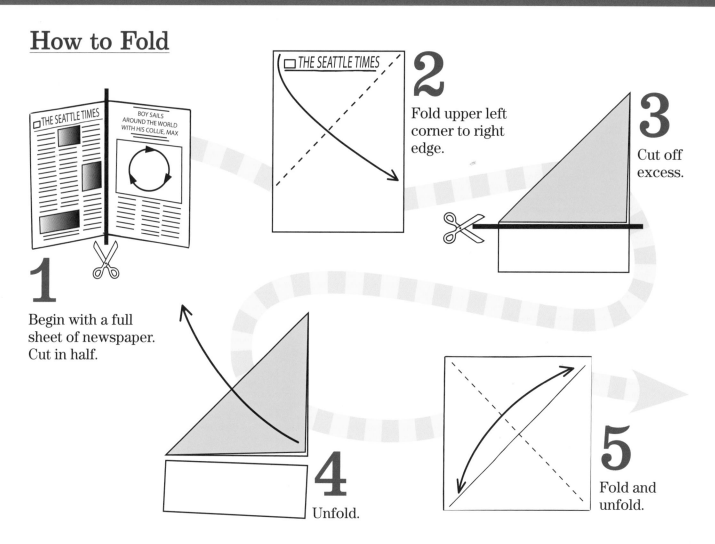

1 Begin with a full sheet of newspaper. Cut in half.

2 Fold upper left corner to right edge.

3 Cut off excess.

4 Unfold.

5 Fold and unfold.

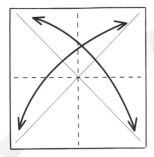

6

Fold and unfold in
both directions.

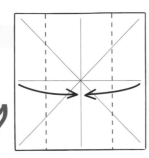

7

Fold both sides to
center crease.

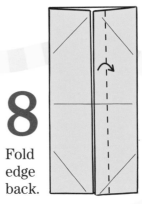

8

Fold
edge
back.

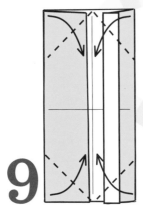

9

Fold all four corners to
center crease.

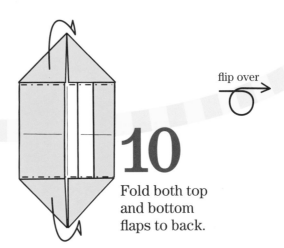

flip over

10

Fold both top
and bottom
flaps to back.

11

Fold and unfold.

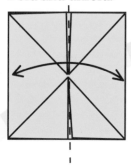

12

Tuck flaps into pockets.

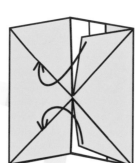

flip over

rotate

13

Insert doo dads into pockets.

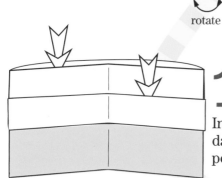

SOUVENIR TRAVEL WALLET

Stunt Plane

Up, up, and away! Have you ever watched a plane streak across the sky? Of course you have. Ever wondered where it is going? Who's on board? Ever marveled how it flies without flapping its wings like a bird? Aeronautics, the science of flight, teaches us that flight is a balance of four forces: thrust, lift, drag, and gravity. Thanks to the Wright Brothers, these four forces were finessed to mechanical perfection in 1903. To celebrate their genius and your trip, try folding this Stunt Plane. Experiment with how you angle the wings, and how you toss it in the air. How aerodynamic can you make it? Caution: Don't test your origami plane while you're 38,000 feet in the air. The folks sitting in front of you might not appreciate a paper plane landing on top of their heads!

The World's Biggest Fly-In!

If you love crazy folks and their crazy kids and their even crazier flying machines, then chart a course to the Experimental Aircraft Association's Fly-In Convention in Oshkosh, Wisconsin. Every summer, more than 10,000 aircraft from all over the world fly to Oshkosh for this amazing aeronautic event. There are concept planes, vintage planes, jets, helicopters, war birds, ultralights, blimps, seaplanes, and aerobatic aircraft. The convention offers seminars, lectures, and even a special kid-friendly tent where you can build your own model plane or learn to fly in a flight simulator. Come to Oshkosh where the Spirit of Flight lives on.

WRIGHT BROTHERS

KITTY HAWK, N.C.

Orville and Wilbur Wright flew their first "flying machine" in 1903 over the sandy plains of Kitty Hawk, North Carolina. The flight only lasted 12 seconds, but it was the first controlled, sustained flight in history.

How to Fold

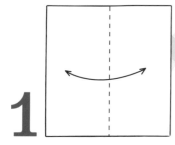

1 Begin with the paper's white side facing up. Fold in half. Unfold.

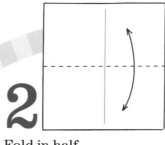

2 Fold in half. Unfold.

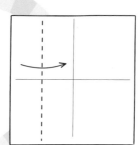

3 Fold left side to center crease.

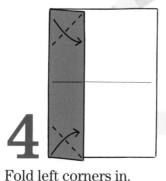

4 Fold left corners in.

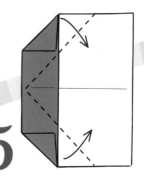

5 Fold left corners to center crease.

Folding the Stunt Plane

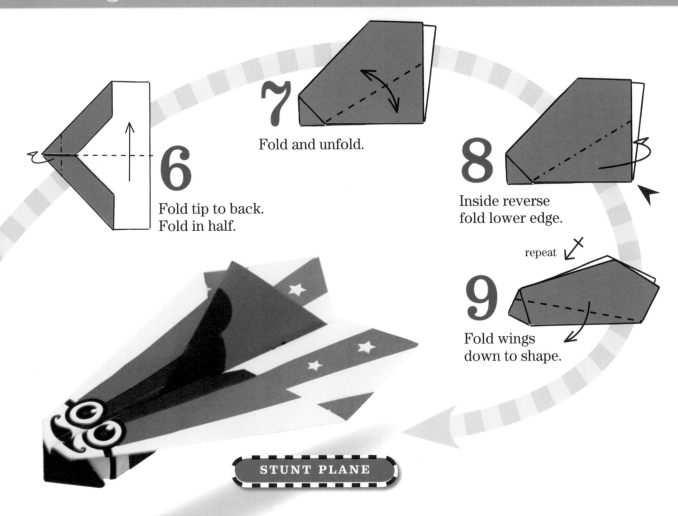

6 Fold tip to back.
Fold in half.

7 Fold and unfold.

8 Inside reverse
fold lower edge.

repeat

9 Fold wings
down to shape.

STUNT PLANE

Want to Play Flying Dice?

Have a little time on your hands while you wait for your plane to depart or your cruise ship to cast off? Fold some paper dice, then play a fun little game of Flying Dice with your traveling companions.

How to Fold

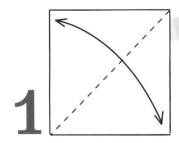

1 Begin with the paper's white side up. Fold and unfold.

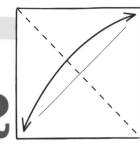

2 Fold and unfold.

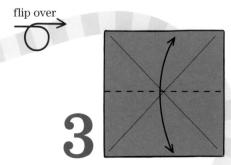

flip over

3 Fold and unfold.

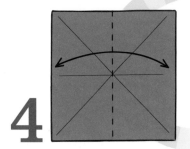

4 Fold and unfold.

flip over

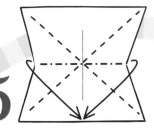

5 Collapse sides inward, and flatten.

6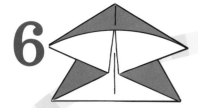

7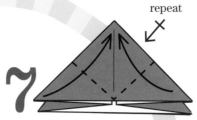

repeat

Fold to center, top
layers only. Repeat
on other side.

8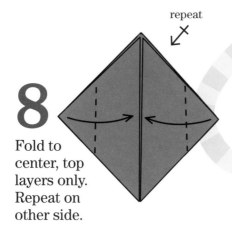

repeat

Fold to
center, top
layers only.
Repeat on
other side.

9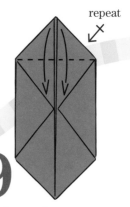

repeat

Fold tips down.
Repeat on other side.

Folding the Flying Dice

repeat

10

Fold and then tuck tips into tiny pockets. Repeat on other side.

No-Tears Tip

Problems inflating? Insert the tip of a pencil into the opening. Then try to inflate.

11

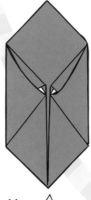

To inflate, hold model gently and blow strongly into the small opening.

blow

FLYING DICE

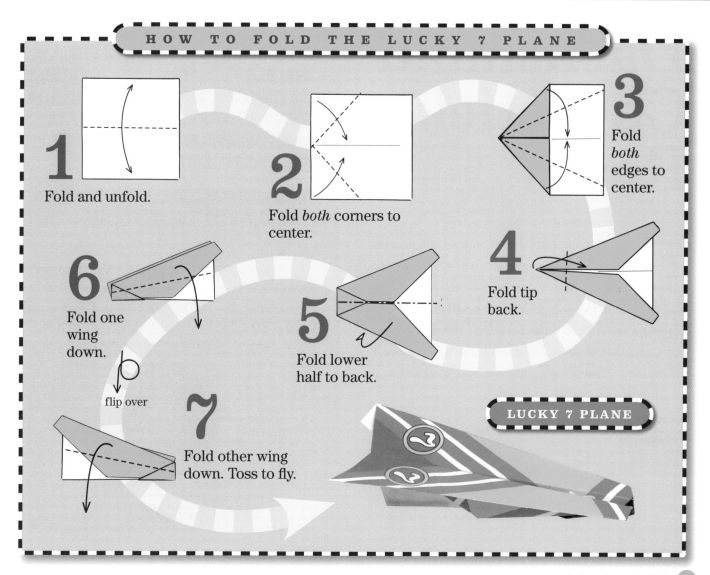

HOW TO FOLD THE LUCKY 7 PLANE

1 Fold and unfold.

2 Fold *both* corners to center.

3 Fold *both* edges to center.

4 Fold tip back.

5 Fold lower half to back.

6 Fold one wing down.

flip over

7 Fold other wing down. Toss to fly.

LUCKY 7 PLANE

Dachshund Chopstick Rest

Did you know that Chinese food can be found in just about every corner of the world? Whether you're flying into Barcelona or Boston, Florence or Flagstaff, you can expect to find your favorite sweet-and-sour chicken dishes or vegetable chow mein at just about any Chinese restaurant in the world. While you're waiting for the bamboo box of steaming tasty treats to arrive, here's a fun little project you can fold. Start by carefully taking the wrapper off your chopsticks, then follow the instructions. Not only will you recycle the wrapper into a convenient resting place for your chopsticks, but you'll have made a cute little dachshund, too.

WORDS OF WISDOM

Learning the local lingo is always appreciated when traveling in a foreign land. A friendly smile and a chirpy "Ciao" will surely light up the face of any Roman citizen. Don't let pronunciation stop you from giving it a try. The locals are always willing to help out. Just repeat after them. Practice does make for a perfect trip.

ENGLISH	hello	good-bye	please	thank you
SPANISH	hola *(o-lah)*	adios *(ah-dee-yose)*	por favor *(por fah-vor)*	gracias *(grah-syas)*
FRENCH	bonjour *(bawn joor)*	au revoir *(aw-reh-vwah)*	s'il vous plaît *(see-voo-play)*	merci *(mare-see)*
GERMAN	Guten Tag *(gooten-tag)*	Auf Wiedersehen *(off wee-der-sayn)*	Bitte *(bitta)*	Danke *(donka)*
ITALIAN	ciao *(chow)*	arrivederci *(ah-reev-ah-durchi)*	per favore *(pair-fah-vor-reh)*	grazie *(grah-tzee)*

How to Fold

Start with a paper chopstick wrapper.

1 Fold in half. Unfold.

2 Fold all four corners to center crease.

3 Fold to center crease.

4

flip over

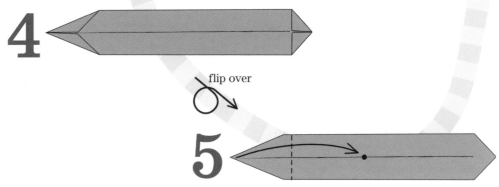

5 Fold to center—approximately.

6

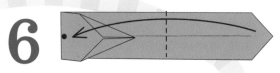

Fold in half.

7

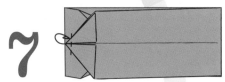

Fold tip back.

flip over

8

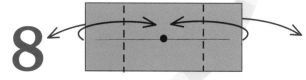

Fold to center, while
flaps on back side
come to front.

9

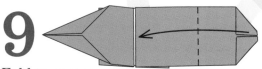

Fold to center.

12

Fold entire model in half.

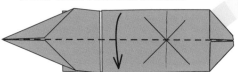

11

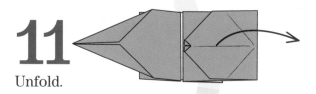

Unfold.

10

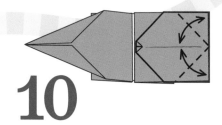

Fold to center. Unfold.

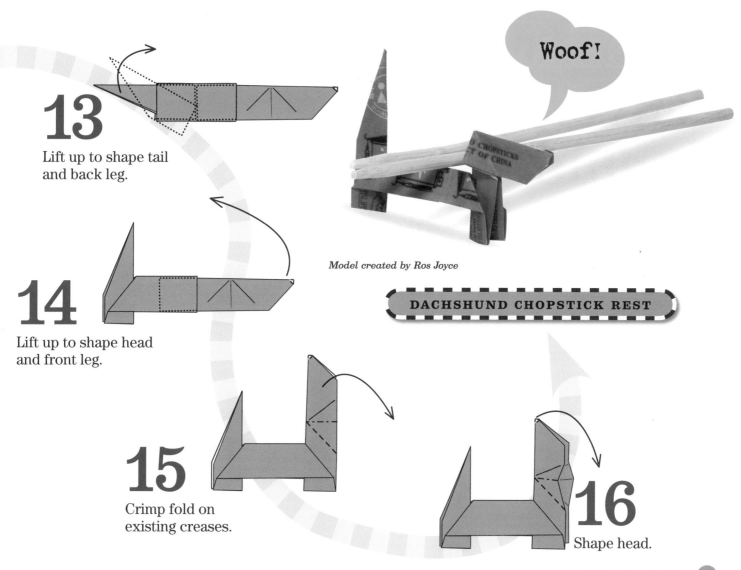

13 Lift up to shape tail and back leg.

Woof!

Model created by Ros Joyce

14 Lift up to shape head and front leg.

DACHSHUND CHOPSTICK REST

15 Crimp fold on existing creases.

16 Shape head.

Snail Mail, Envelope Included

Are you going to be away for more than a few days? Want to send a letter to a friend back home? Grab a sheet of paper and write a note on one side, then follow the folding instructions and your letter will be ready to send. No separate envelope needed, but you may need extra postage. Any sheet of letter-size paper will do, and if you are overseas, a sheet of A4 works well, too.

*WARNING: Try not to brag too much in your note. Remember, your friends are having a normal day at home, eating their ordinary food, sleeping in their regular beds, walking down their familiar sidewalks. Gosh, don't you just *love* to travel?

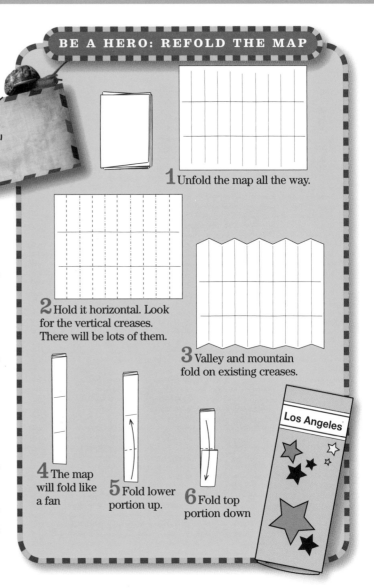

BE A HERO: REFOLD THE MAP

1 Unfold the map all the way.

2 Hold it horizontal. Look for the vertical creases. There will be lots of them.

3 Valley and mountain fold on existing creases.

4 The map will fold like a fan

5 Fold lower portion up.

6 Fold top portion down

Los Angeles

How to Fold

Start with a sheet of letter-size paper.

1

Dear Josh,

The surf is up!

The Hawaiian

Punch is yummy.

Wish you were here.

Sven

Begin with the paper's
white side facing up.
Fold in half. Unfold.

2

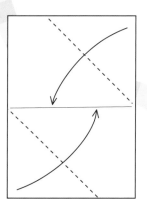

Fold top and bottom
corners to center crease.

rotate

3

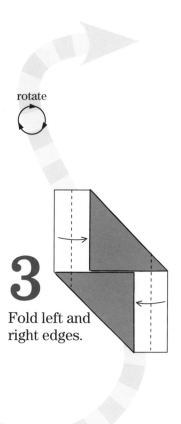

Fold left and
right edges.

Folding Snail Mail, Envelope Included

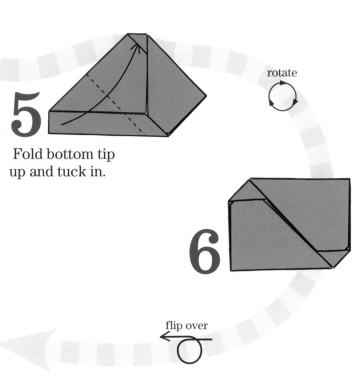

4 Fold top tip down and tuck in.

5 Fold bottom tip up and tuck in.

rotate

6

flip over

SNAIL MAIL WITH ENVELOPE

TO: JOSH JONAS
West 81st Street
New York, NY 10024

Tiny Scrapbook

MOUNT EVEREST
HIMALAYAS

SKY HIGH

Set up base camp at foot of Mount Everest today. Can't believe I'm in the Himalayas! I mean, the peak of Everest is THE TALLEST PLACE ON EARTH! 29,035 feet high!

When you travel, you want to remember every hour, every minute, every second, every blink of your trip, but it's not always easy to keep track of time. You might be jet-lagged, or seeing so many places that your memories get jumbled together. During your trip, you might have experienced days that were so peaceful and beautiful that you want to hang onto them forever. Maybe you were out on a hike one day, the bright blue sky and puffy white clouds above you, and on the trail you saw the most amazing redwood tree, so tall you almost fell over looking up at it. If you had a scrapbook with you—a tiny scrapbook—you could make a quick sketch, jot down a few words, collect a pine needle—and capture the beauty of that scene forever. Later, when you look at the scrapbook's pages, you'll remember just how wonderful the day was.

The Himalayas is a mountain range located on the border between Nepal and Tibet, China.

How to Fold

1 Begin with a sheet of copy paper. Fold in half. Unfold.

2 Fold in half. Unfold.

3 Fold and unfold both sides to center crease. Unfold.

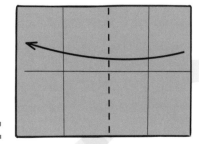

4 Fold in half.

6

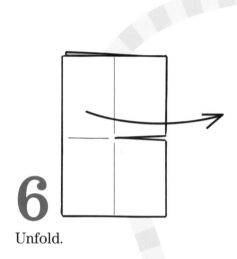

Unfold.

7

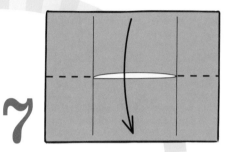

Fold in half.

8

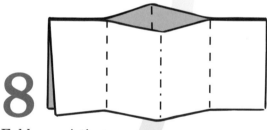

Fold on existing
creases.

5

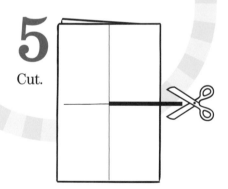

Cut!

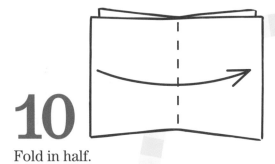

10

Fold in half.

TINY SCRAPBOOK

9

Arrange pages/flaps right and left.

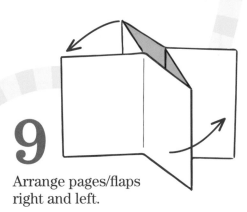

Raccoon Finger Puppet

Finger puppets make for great impromptu entertainment—especially if you have a little brother or sister you'd like to amuse. Why not put on a show? Fold a finger puppet and make up a story. This cute little raccoon finger puppet will surely delight. When the word gets out, you may end up performing for a shipload of fans.

Berlin, Germany

RACCOONS

These masked little rascals are extremely curious and lead very active lives. They have adapted to a wide variety of habitats, from the desert, to pine forests, near lakes and streams, to urban areas. Native to North America, raccoons were introduced into Germany in the 1930s, and can now be found throughout much of Western Europe. One especially inquisitive raccoon even took up residence in a hotel—in the middle of Berlin! Unfortunately for the patrons of the hotel, raccoons are nocturnal, which means they snooze during the day and get into mischief at night, when everyone is trying to sleep.

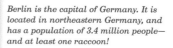

Berlin is the capital of Germany. It is located in northeastern Germany, and has a population of 3.4 million people— and at least one raccoon!

How to Fold

Start with a quarter sheet
of raccoon paper.

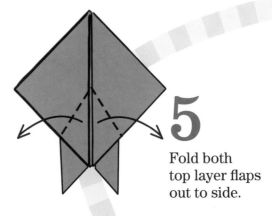

1

Begin with
the paper's
white side
facing up.
Fold in half.

2

3

Fold top edge
down about
½ inch.

4

Fold both tips
down to center.

5

Fold both
top layer flaps
out to side.

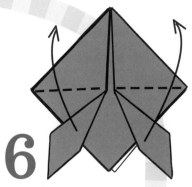

6

Fold flaps up.

7

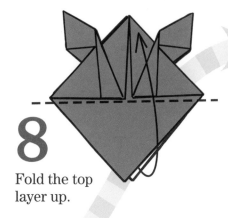

8

Fold the top layer up.

Folding the Raccoon Finger Puppet

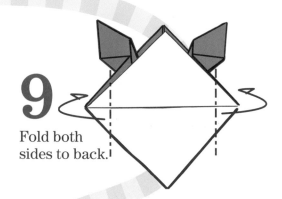

9 Fold both sides to back.

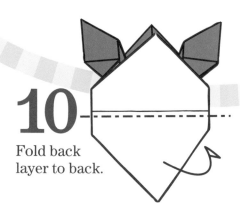

10 Fold back layer to back.

11 Insert finger into pocket. It's show time . . .

Pig Finger Puppet

The Back Seat Theatre (that's you) is looking for a new musical act. How about making several pig finger puppets—one for each finger on your hand? It could be a performing pig family: The Sensational Singing Swine! Pinky Swine sings a solo and has the sweetest little voice. The crowd goes hog wild, cheering for Pinky to sing just one more. Okay, it's not exactly Shakespeare, but it sure is fun!

STRATFORD-UPON-AVON

SHAKESPEARE

E N G L A N D

Stratford

Shakespeare Country

Are you visiting England in your travels? If so, head to Stratford-upon-Avon, birthplace of the ultrafamous playwright and poet William Shakespeare. You know Will, right? Author of *Romeo and Juliet*, *Hamlet*, *Macbeth* (and countless other plays)? Well, if you've never seen a Shakespearean play, you might want to check out a performance by the Royal Shakespeare Company. Based in Stratford-upon-Avon, it's one of the best-known theatre companies in the world.

How to Fold

Start with a quarter
sheet of pig paper.

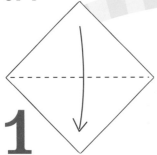

1 Begin with the
paper's white side
facing up. Fold in half.

2

3 Fold both tips
down to center.

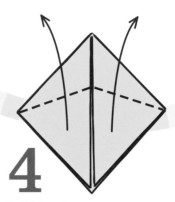

4 Fold both
flaps of top layer
up, just off center.

5

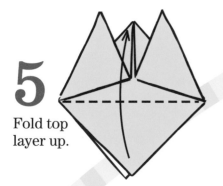

Fold top
layer up.

6

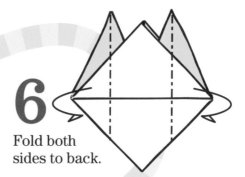

Fold both
sides to back.

7

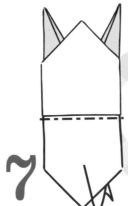

Fold back
layer to top.

8

Fold tip of head
to back.

Folding the Pig Finger Puppet

9

Outside reverse
fold ear.

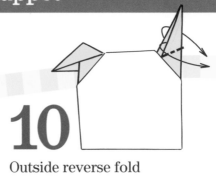

10

Outside reverse fold
other ear.

11

Fold tips of
ears to the
inside.

PIG FINGER PUPPETS

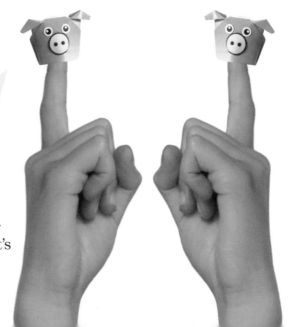

12

Insert finger
into pocket. It's
show time!

Fortune Teller

Do you have questions? Need answers but don't know whom to ask? For a little help, you might consider folding a Fortune Teller so you can get instant answers to the silliest of questions. Ask it whatever question pops into your head. Will Mom get a speeding ticket today? Should I wear a raincoat tomorrow? Does my dog miss me? Just ask the Fortune Teller. Keep it in your pocket in case you come to a crossroads and don't know which way to turn.

The Fortune Teller whispers,

"Look in the back of your book to find special fortune-telling paper. If you run out, the spirits will help you make your own."

TREVI FOUNTAIN • ITALY • ROME •

LOOKING FOR LUCK?

What is it about the sight of a fountain that makes us dig into our pockets to find a coin, make a wish, and toss the coin into the water? If you want to increase your luck by making wishes, then you should head either to Rome, Italy, or Kansas City, Missouri. Both cities claim to have more fountains than any other place on the planet.

Rome, of course, is home to the famous Trevi Fountain, which is easily the most famous fountain in the world. Legend has it that if you toss a coin into the Trevi, you are guaranteed to return to this romantic spot in the future.

Kansas City has the famous JC Nichols Memorial Fountain, with four rearing horses that represent the four major rivers of the world: the Mississippi (U.S.), the Volga (Russian Federation), the Seine (France), and the Rhine (Germany). Now, make a wish.

Kansas City is the largest city in Missouri, a state in the Midwestern region of the U.S.A.

Kansas City

Rome

Rome is not only the largest city in Italy, it is the capital. Over two and a half thousand years old, it is one of the oldest cities in Western civilization.

Origami on the Go! **41**

Folding the Fortune Teller

How to Fold

1 Begin with the paper's white side facing up. Fold and unfold in both directions.

2 Fold and unfold in both directions.

3 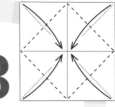 Fold corners to center.

4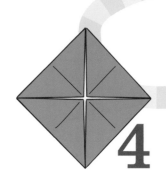

 flip over

5  Write eight different fortunes in the areas between the creases.

6 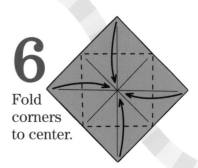 Fold corners to center.

To find out your fortune, pick a number between 1 and 8. Count as you open and shut model desired number of times. Now pick one of the four stars inside the model. Open up that flap to reveal your fortune.

Here are a few fortune ideas to get your imagination going . . .

1. Positively *YES*
2. Your wish is granted
3. Watch out for the person on your left
4. Ask again later
5. Look for more clues
6. Listen carefully to those around you
7. Bring Band-aids
8. Wear a hat

FORTUNE TELLER

10

Fold up so stars are hidden inside and eyes are visible outside.

flip over

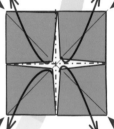

9

To shape model, open up flaps and insert fingers.

8

Draw spooky eyes on each flap.

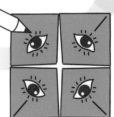

flip over

7

Draw eight stars in areas between the creases.

Jumping Frog Business Card

This high-flying froggie is a real crowd pleaser. Whether young or old, boy or girl, princess or pirate—everyone loves this model. You can fold it from a business card or an index card, and even a postcard will work if you don't mind a low jumper. You can pick up a business card at almost any shop or restaurant, but don't take more than one—that's just beastly.

The 700,00 or so Cajuns who live in Louisiana are descendents of French Canadians, who had established a colony in Nova Scotia in 1604. For rebelling against British rule, they were forced from their homes in 1755, and resettled in the bayous (swamps, creeks, rivers) of southern Louisiana.

Louisiana
(Cajun Country)

LOUISIANA CAJUN FRIED FROG LEGS

A real Cajun cook starts preparing meals the night before. Armed with a flashlight, a sack, and a stick called a *gig*, the cook will head out to look for the main ingredient of a favorite dish: Cajun Fried Frog Legs. It used to be that chefs had to hunt for these tasty jumpers, but today frogs are raised on farms, just like chickens and turkeys. Back in the kitchen, the chef dips the frog legs in an egg batter, and then coats them in a spicy flour-cornmeal mixture. Next the frog legs are fried, much like chicken. This dish is a real double dare because fried frog legs are always served as a pair. Yikes!

How to Fold

Start with a business card.

1

Begin with the information side facing up. Fold and unfold.

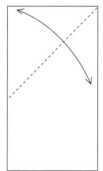

2

Fold and unfold.

flip over

3

Fold and unfold.

flip over

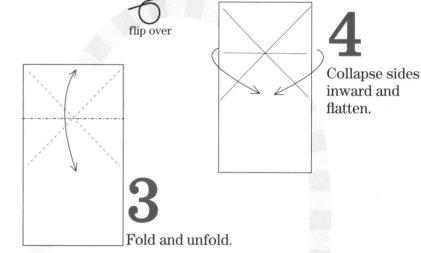

4

Collapse sides inward and flatten.

5

Fold top tips of top layer up.

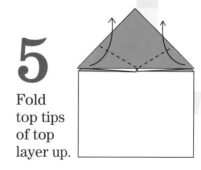

7 Fold bottom edge to top tip.

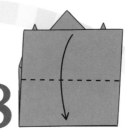

8 Fold top layer down.

flip over

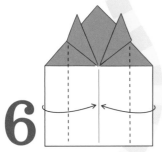

6 Fold sides to center.

margaret van sicklen

9 Frog will jump when given a quick flick.

JUMPING FROG BUSINESS CARD

Knick-knack Box

You should always be prepared to leave your hotel room at a moment's notice. What if you hear the sound of a marching band, or see an amazing rainbow out the window? Or maybe your entire family overslept and now you're all scrambling to make it to the breakfast buffet in time. You have to be ready to grab your camera and go! Fold this little box to help keep yourself organized. Keep your spare change inside. Lip balm. Wristbands. Hair ties. Don't be surprised if you have to fold a couple of extras for your parents and/or siblings.

According to a recent survey of world travelers, the top ten favorite cities to visit are:

High Five to the Top Ten

1. Bangkok, Thailand
2. Buenos Aires, Argentina
3. Cape Town, South Africa
4. Sydney, Australia
5. Florence, Italy
6. Cuzco, Peru
7. Rome, Italy
8. New York, U.S.A.
9. Istanbul, Turkey
10. San Francisco, U.S.A.

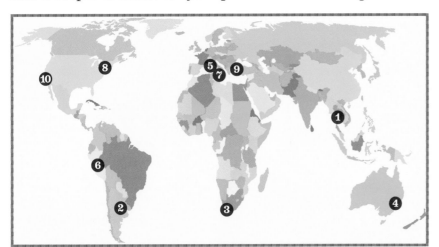

Folding the Knick-knack Box

How to Fold

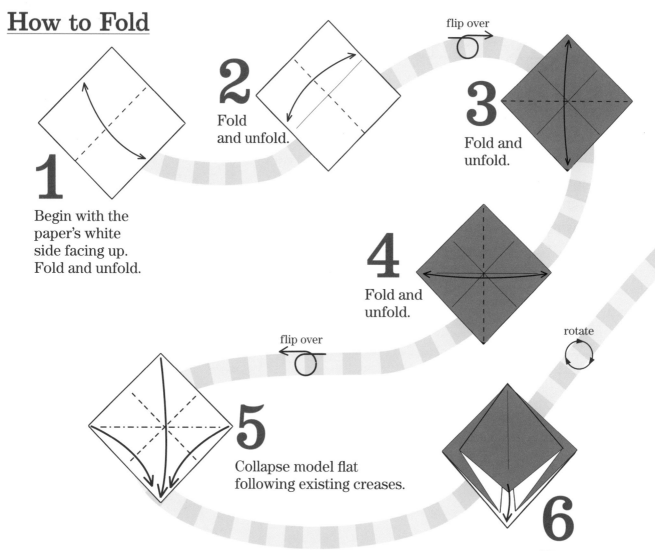

1 Begin with the paper's white side facing up. Fold and unfold.

2 Fold and unfold.

flip over

3 Fold and unfold.

4 Fold and unfold.

flip over

5 Collapse model flat following existing creases.

rotate

6 Flatten into a square.

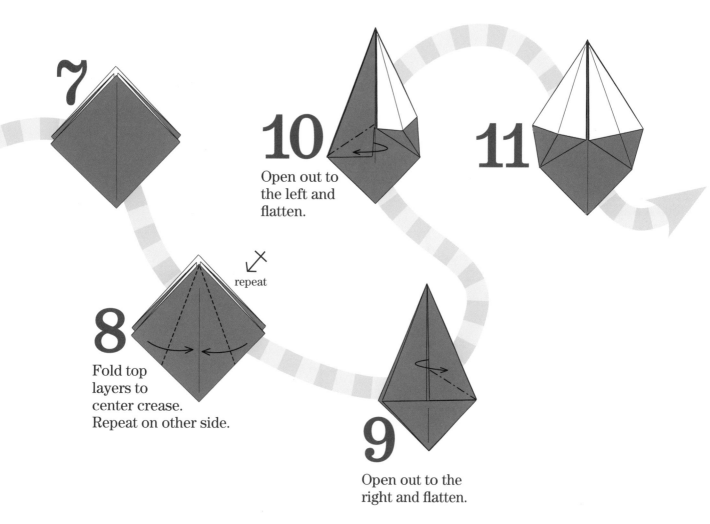

7

8 Fold top layers to center crease. Repeat on other side.

repeat

9 Open out to the right and flatten.

10 Open out to the left and flatten.

11

Folding the Knick-knack Box

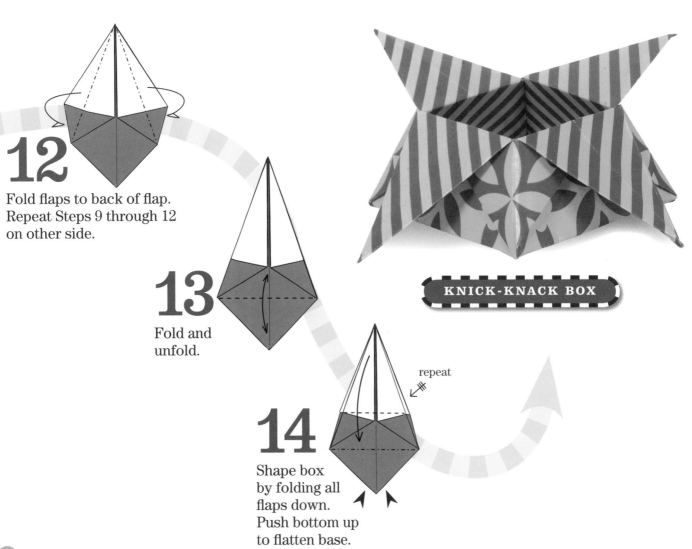

12 Fold flaps to back of flap. Repeat Steps 9 through 12 on other side.

13 Fold and unfold.

14 Shape box by folding all flaps down. Push bottom up to flatten base.

repeat

KNICK-KNACK BOX

Million-Dollar Bow Tie

P lans are always changing when you travel. You always have to be ready for an upgrade. One minute you're checking out the World's Largest Cowboy Boot, and the next you're getting dolled up to dine. With this little model up your sleeve, you're instantly dressed up. Girls, you can pin it on your top or wear it in your hair. When a tie is a must for the gentleman, go classic with this bow tie. You can look like a million bucks and it won't even cost a penny.

Origami, International Style

A re you traveling to Finland, Argentina, Poland, or Peru? The love of paper folding can be found around the globe. Folders are always happy to meet other folders, and they welcome visitors to their monthly meetings and annual conventions.

Check out OrigamiUSA for a current list of international groups at **www.origami-usa.org.** There may be a group closer than you think!

How to Fold

1 Begin with a dollar bill face up. Fold in half. Unfold.

2 Fold back to center crease.

3 Fold right side behind.

4 Fold in half.

5 Open up top flap. Flatten corner gently into a triangle.

6 Inside reverse fold lower corner.

7 Lift top flap.

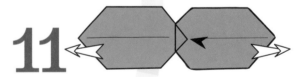

MILLION-DOLLAR BOW TIE

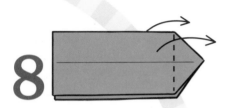

8
Fold top flap all the way over. Repeat on other side.

repeat

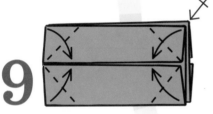

9
Fold all four corners to center. Repeat on other side.

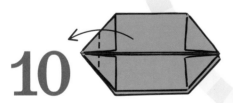

10
Fold top flap to the left.

11
To shape center, gently pull both sides.

Heart Place Card

Are you getting together with family and friends while you're traveling? Perhaps you are going to a birthday party or a family reunion. Why don't you offer to help decorate the table to make it look more festive? These little heart-shaped place cards are folded very easily, and are always a welcoming sight at any table. After folding, write each person's name on the front of the card and put it at a place setting. It's a great way to arrange the seating so you can sit next to your favorite people.

The OK Hint

Is his my water glass? Is that your bread plate or mine? Have you ever been in the situation where you can't figure out which bread plate is yours? Here's a handy trick to help you remember. Make an OK sign with both your right and left hands. Now look at your left hand: It looks like a lowercase "b" as in "bread." Your right hand resembles a lowercase "d" as in "drink. " Your bread plate is on the left and your drinking glass is on the right. Now you'll never be confused again.

How to Fold

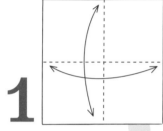

1 Begin with the paper's white side facing up. Fold and unfold in both directions.

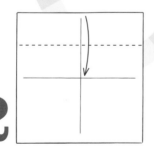

2 Fold top edge to the center crease.

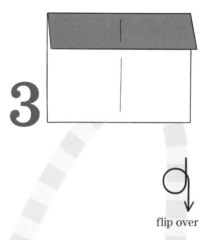

3

flip over

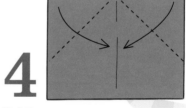

4 Fold top corners to center crease.

Folding the Heart Place Card

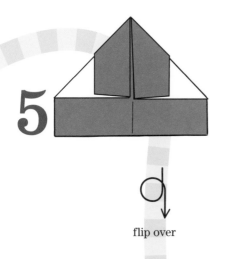

5

flip over

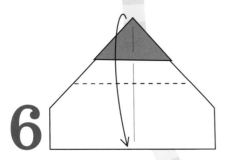

6

Fold tip to crease at bottom edge.

flip over

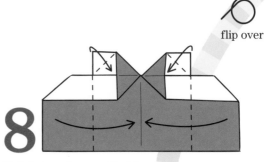

flip over

8

Fold tips down. Fold the sides to center.

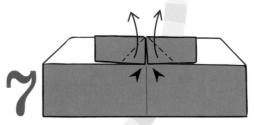

7

Lift flaps and squash flat.

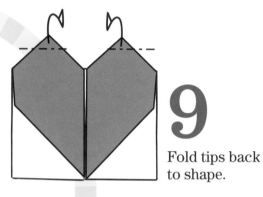

9

Fold tips back to shape.

10

To stand model up, fold sides back.

HEART PLACE CARD

X Marks the Spot

If you look at a world map or a globe, you will notice horizontal and vertical lines that form an imaginary grid. The lines are called latitude and longitude, and they are used to pinpoint a geographical location. Latitudinal lines run north and south of the equator. They are also called parallels, because they circle the planet like a series of parallel belts that never touch each other. Longitudinal lines, which are vertical, run from North Pole to South Pole, dividing the Earth into sections like an orange. There are 360 longitudinal lines—180 to the east and 180 to the west of the prime meridian. This is the line that divides the eastern hemisphere from the western hemisphere, and it's located in Greenwich, England. Using longitude and latitude coordinates, travelers know their exact location anywhere on the planet. So if you ever happen to find yourself at 43°N 13' 56", 108° E 8' 19" you'll know you're in the middle of the Gobi Desert in Mongolia.

HINT: To help you remember which is which, latitude sounds a bit like ladder; so imagine the rungs of a ladder. And longitude sounds loooong, like the long lines stretching from north to south.

PART TWO

Hoofed, Horned, or Hairy, We Love Them All

We share the planet with amazing, amusing, and adorable creatures. Animals live in the mountains, in the grasslands, underwater, underground, and in the sky.

They live where it is super hot and super cold, super dry and soaking wet. They have perfectly adapted to living in almost every habitat on Earth. Some animals have extra thick, water-repellent fur that keeps them comfortable in the rain, and some have specially shaped feet that make them excellent swimmers. Others have extra curly lashes to keep the sand out of their eyes, or eyes that let them see in the dark. Still others have special ears that allow them to hear the faintest sounds from a long way off. Some animals even have pockets in which they carry their young. Animals come in small, medium, large, and extra large, and in every color of the rainbow. In all corners of the world, if you keep your eyes peeled, you can find the most amazing creatures. And we love them *all*!

Iowa Piggy

I f the sight of a curly tail and a wet snout makes your heart race, then ask the navigator to set the GPS for Des Moines, Iowa (41°N 35' 45", 93°W 32' 53"). There, in August, the Iowa State Fair is buzzing with pig pride. Don't forget your camera—these cuties are very photogenic. You'll see award-winning Spotted Swine, Hampshire Hogs, and lots and lots of other breeds, all washed, brushed, and polished to pig perfection.

DES MOINES
IOWA

What's in a Name?

D es Moines was founded in 1843 by Captain James Allen, who built a fort on the site where the Des Moines River merged into the Raccoon River. Luckily for Iowans, Allen didn't use the name Fort Raccoon for his new settlement. If he had, the capital of Iowa might have been called Raccoon instead of Des Moines!

Des Moines is the capital of Iowa, a state in the Midwest region of the U.S.A. The state was named for the Ioway people, a Native American tribe that had lived there.

Des Moines, Iowa

How to Fold

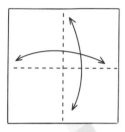

1 Begin with the paper's white side facing up. Fold and unfold in both directions.

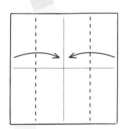

2 Fold sides to center crease.

rotate

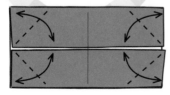

3 Fold and unfold all corners.

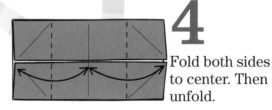

4 Fold both sides to center. Then unfold.

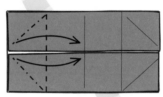

5 Fold top layer back to center crease.

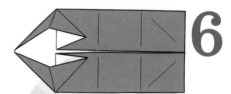

6

Folding the Iowa Piggy

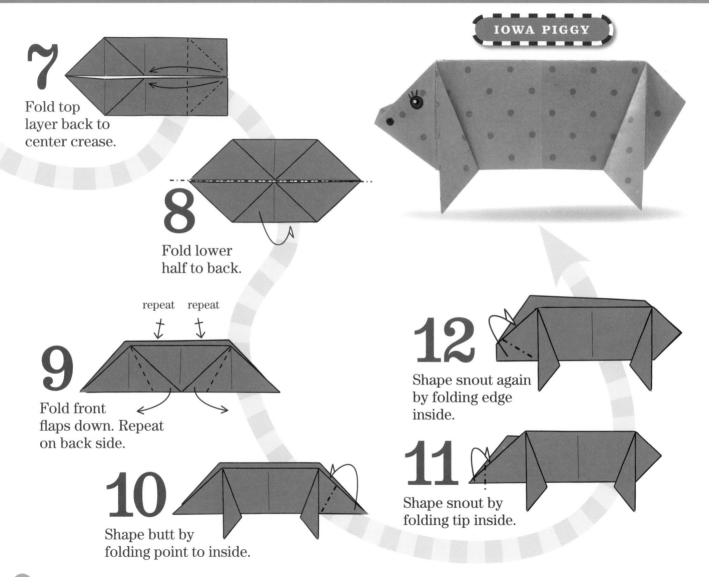

7 Fold top layer back to center crease.

IOWA PIGGY

8 Fold lower half to back.

repeat repeat

9 Fold front flaps down. Repeat on back side.

12 Shape snout again by folding edge inside.

11 Shape snout by folding tip inside.

10 Shape butt by folding point to inside.

Malaysia Cicada

What did you say? I can't hear you! When visiting Malaysia, you may need to crank your outside voice up a notch if you want to be heard over the racket made by the cicadas. These incredible bugs are by far the noisiest of all insects. If you want to help keep the noise down, you might consider eating a few. That's right: Cicadas are considered a tasty treat in some parts of the world—a crunchy, protein-filled snack! Do grab a napkin, because they are a bit juicer than you might expect.

Welcome To The Jungle

Taman Negara National Park, located in Pahang, Malaysia, is said to be the oldest jungle still in existence today. It survived because the Ice Ages didn't reach this area. Originally accessible only by riverboat, this pristine rainforest is the real deal. And in a jungle with vegetation as dense as this, you might pass right by an exotic reptile and not even notice it. What you will notice are hundreds of species of birds, butterflies, and more insects than you have ever imagined possible. The jungle is literally crawling with them.

Let's hear a cheer for six legs!! Click, click, hooray! Click, click, hooray!

Malaysia is a country in Southeast Asia. It borders Thailand, Indonesia, Singapore, Brunei, and the Philippines. Since it is located near the equator, Malaysia's climate is tropical.

How to Fold

1 Begin with the paper's white side facing up. Fold in half. Unfold.

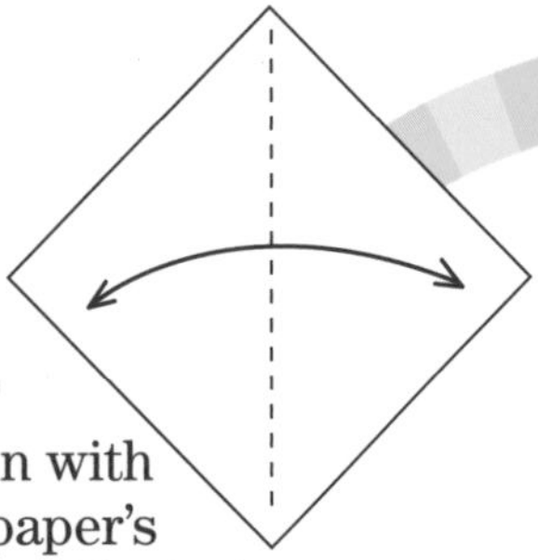

2 Fold in half.

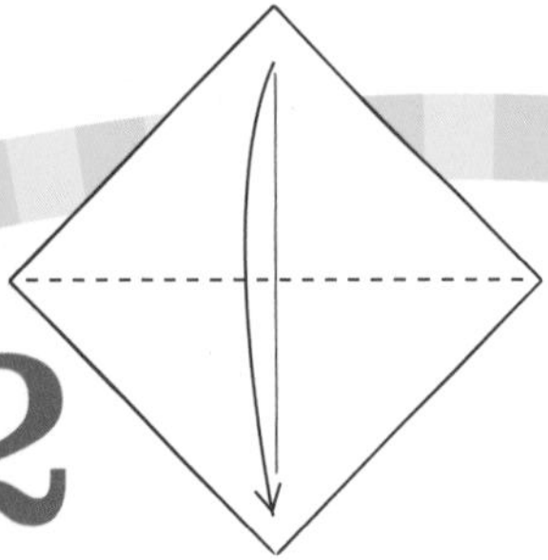

3 Fold right side to center crease.

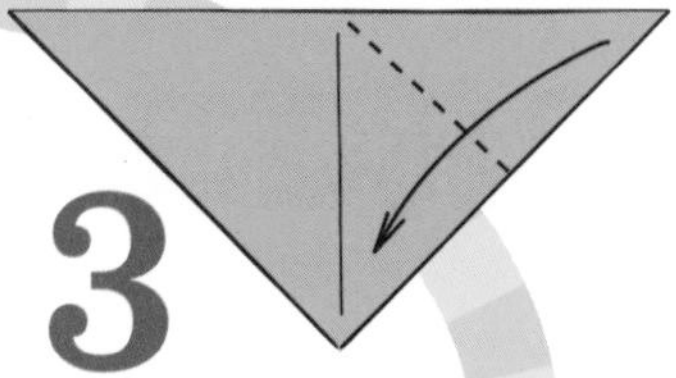

4 Fold left side to center crease.

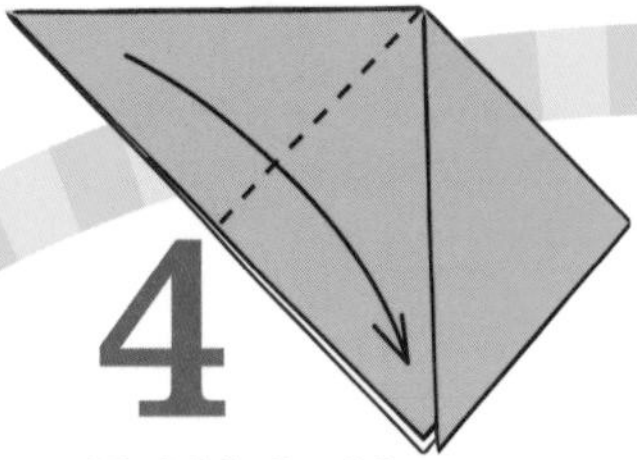

5

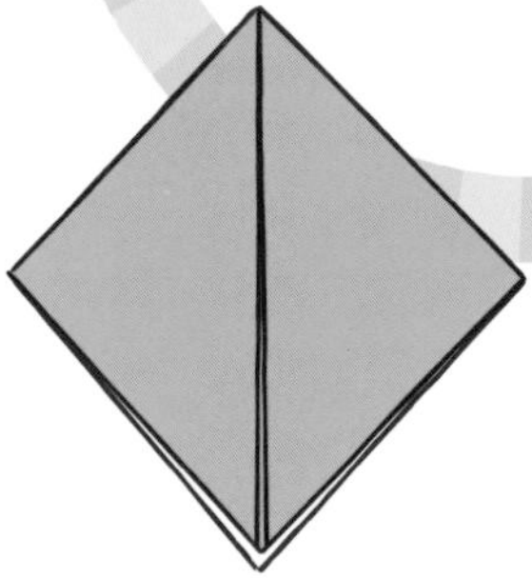

rotate

6 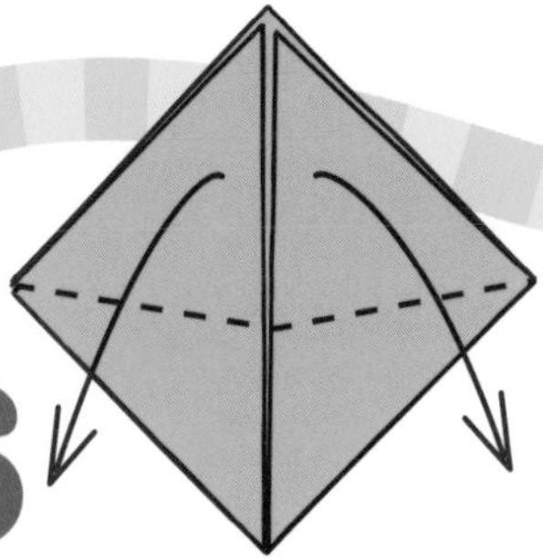 Fold the top layer of both flaps down, just off center.

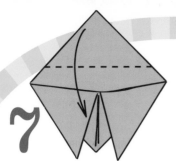

7 Fold top layer down.

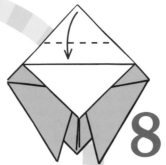

8 Fold back layer down.

9 Fold both sides to back.

MALAYSIA CICADA

New Zealand Rabbit

With their soft fur, twitching noses, and long ears, rabbits are hard to resist. Who on this Earth doesn't love a rabbit? Well, don't tell that to New Zealanders, who know a lot about these crafty tricksters. First released into the wilds of New Zealand in 1777 by the famous explorer James Cook, rabbits quickly outwitted all their local enemies and basically took over New Zealand. Nothing—not even humans—could stop those ferocious bunnies from gobbling up the New Zealand crops. So be careful around rabbits: They will chew on anything—even your favorite sneakers!

International Date Line

The International Date Line sits a little crooked on the 180° longitude line in the Pacific Ocean east of New Zealand. This is where the calendar day ends and a new day begins. The line is not perfectly straight, as it has been shifted to accommodate the many island countries in that region. So if your birthday is January 28, let's say, and you want to double your fun, start the celebration in Fiji. Then, after dinner, jump on a plane and fly east to Samoa, where it will still be the evening of January 27. Have a good night's sleep, and start the festivities all over again the next morning.

New Zealand is located in the southwestern Pacific Ocean, about 1,250 miles southeast of Australia. It is an island country with a very varied topography consisting of dense forests, tall mountains, volcanoes, and beaches.

How to Fold

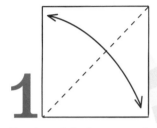

1 Begin with the paper's white side facing up. Fold and unfold.

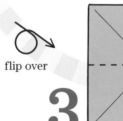

2 Fold and unfold.

flip over

3 Fold and unfold.

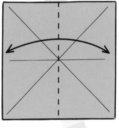

4 Fold and unfold.

flip over

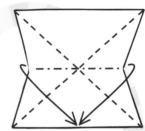

5 Tap center. Collapse sides inward, and flatten.

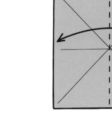

6

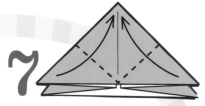

7

Fold to center crease, top layers only.

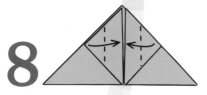

8

Fold tips to center, top layers only.

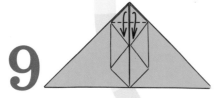

9

Fold tips down.

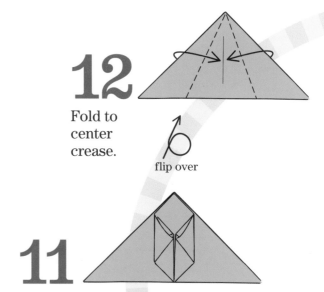

12

Fold to center crease.

flip over

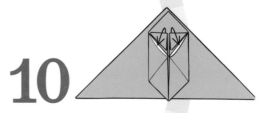

11

10

Fold and then tuck tips into tiny pockets.

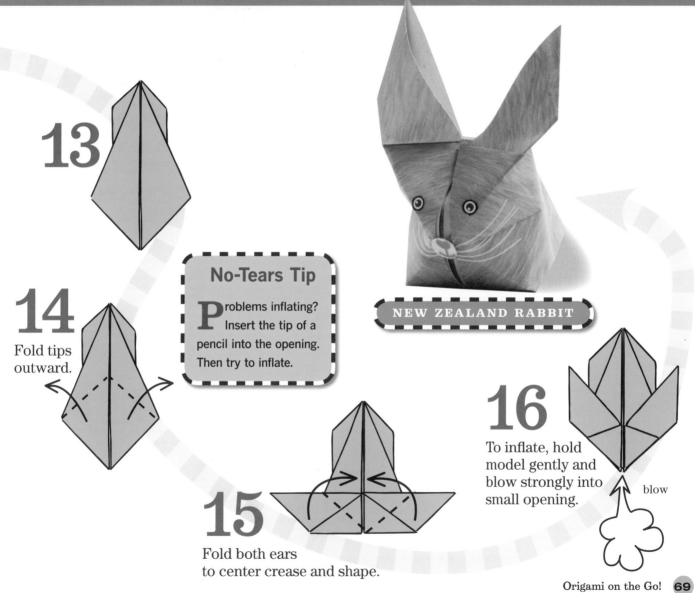

13

14

Fold tips outward.

No-Tears Tip

Problems inflating? Insert the tip of a pencil into the opening. Then try to inflate.

NEW ZEALAND RABBIT

15

Fold both ears to center crease and shape.

16

To inflate, hold model gently and blow strongly into small opening.

blow

Amazon River Turtle

BRAZIL
AMAZON RIVER

Turtles prefer to take its easy. They like a slow, mellow pace. Given how long they've survived on this planet, which they once shared with the dinosaurs, I'd say they've earned a little rest and relaxation. Yellow Spotted Amazon River Turtles have soft supple skin, yellow spots on their heads and necks, and gorgeous large shells measuring fourteen to twenty-seven inches. If you see one of these spotted beauties napping on a rock, please keep your voices down: These ancient creatures don't like surprises. Remember, you're a visitor in their neighborhood, so respect the locals.

Supersize

The Amazon River is considered by most to be the greatest river in the world. It rates as the largest river, carries more water to the ocean than any other river, and sustains millions of different species of wildlife. Things grow bigger there, too. The Amazon water lily has enormous round leaves that can grow to be six to eight feet across, and the anaconda snake can grow to eighteen to twenty feet long. How big is that, you may wonder? Big. Really BIG.

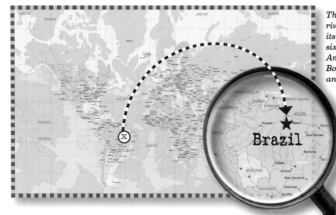

The mouth of the Amazon river is in Brazil, but it or its tributaries run through six other countries of South America: Peru, Colombia, Bolivia, Venezuela, Ecuador, and Guyana.

How to Fold

1 Begin with the paper's color side facing up. Fold in half. Unfold.

2 Fold both sides to center crease.

flip over

3 Bring the folded edges to meet the center crease, allowing the side points underneath to pop out.

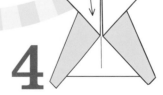

4 Fold top point down.

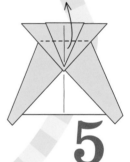

5 Fold the tip upward to create a head.

6 Fold up so that the bottom edge meets vertical center crease.

Folding the Amazon River Turtle

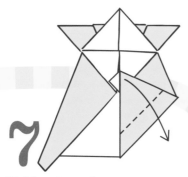

7 Fold outward.

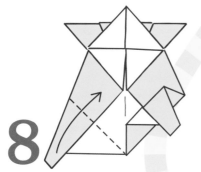

8 Fold up so that the bottom edge meets vertical center crease.

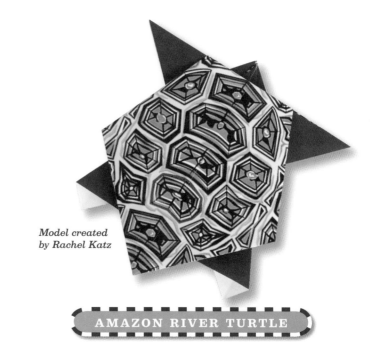

Model created by Rachel Katz

AMAZON RIVER TURTLE

9 Fold outward.

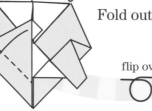

flip over

Antartica Penguin

A re you ready to fold a few penguins? Because folding just one won't do at all: Penguins are highly social creatures and love to hang out together. They swim together, feed together, and even nest together in large groups called *rookeries*. These black and white feathered friends from the south love the snow and ice. That's correct, they live in Antarctica on the edge of the South Pole. Penguins have never resided above the equator. Too bad they never travel to the North Pole; during busy season Santa could sure use the extra help.

Southern Ocean
ANTARCTICA

A Fifth Ocean

In 2000, the International Hydrographic Organization named a fifth world ocean. (Surfers, don't freak: They didn't discover your secret spot!) After much research, scientists felt it was important to redefine the waters that surrounded Antarctica as a separate ecosystem. Now all the southern portions of the Atlantic Ocean, Indian Ocean, and Pacific Ocean have a new name: the Southern Ocean. The penguins applauded.

The South Pole is the southernmost point of the Earth. It is situated on a sheet of ice that is 9,000 feet thick. In the summer, the average temperature on the South Pole is -12°F. In the winter that temperature drops to around -85°F.

Antartica

Name the Oceans

Indian Ocean

Atlantic Ocean

Arctic Ocean

Pacific Ocean

Southern Ocean

Folding the Antarctica Penguin

How to Fold

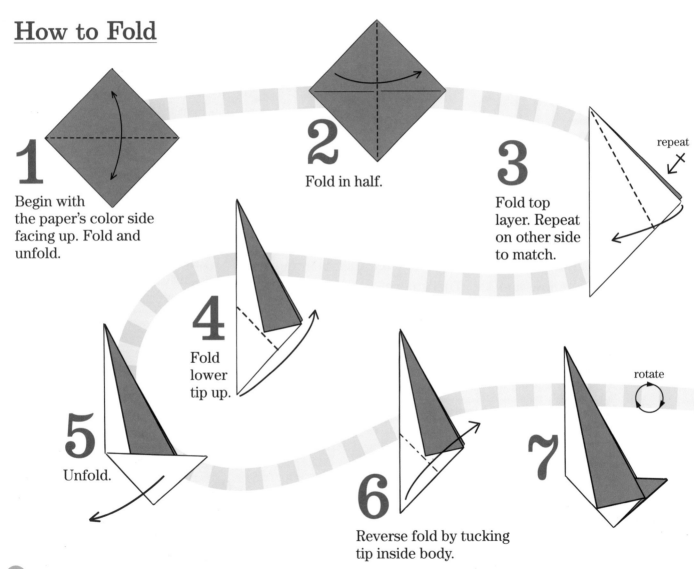

1 Begin with the paper's color side facing up. Fold and unfold.

2 Fold in half.

3 Fold top layer. Repeat on other side to match.

repeat

4 Fold lower tip up.

5 Unfold.

6 Reverse fold by tucking tip inside body.

7

rotate

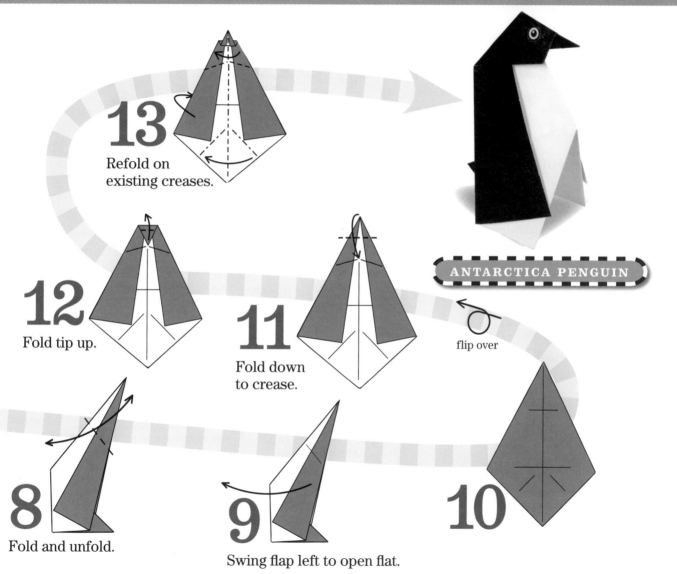

13 Refold on existing creases.

12 Fold tip up.

11 Fold down to crease.

flip over

ANTARCTICA PENGUIN

10

8 Fold and unfold.

9 Swing flap left to open flat.

Grand Canyon Rattlesnake

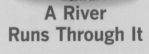

Nothing makes me run faster than the sight of a snake. They have many good qualities, it's true, and many snakes are completely harmless. But still, there's something about them that makes me lose my cool and run away, arms waving in the air, like a total ninny. But why should I like a creature that is constantly sticking its tongue out at me? I saw that! It just did it again!

Slither on over to a map and find the Grand Canyon. Hint: It is located in a hot desert area where snakes like to curl up for a nap.

A River Runs Through It

The Grand Canyon is a 277-mile long gash in the Earth's surface and is more than a mile deep in places. Some 6 million years in the making, this amazing canyon was cut by the mighty Colorado River. When you stand on the edge of the canyon and gaze across to the other side, you will be amazed by the colors of the sandstone. The canyon is so big, it seems unreal. How long is 277 miles? Let's imagine we are going to form a human chain by holding hands with a group of friends. If we assume an average ten-year-old has an arm span of 55 inches, we would need 319,104 kids to stretch out their arms to reach from one end of the canyon to the other. Yikes, that is a lot of kids!

The Grand Canyon is located in the state of Arizona, which is in the southwestern region of the U.S.A. As one of the world's greatest natural wonders, it attracts about five million visitors a year.

How to Fold

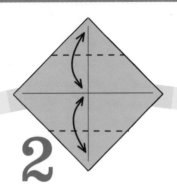

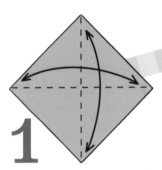

1 Begin with the paper's color side facing up. Fold and unfold in both directions.

2 Fold to center crease and unfold.

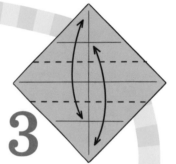

3 Fold corners to creases and unfold.

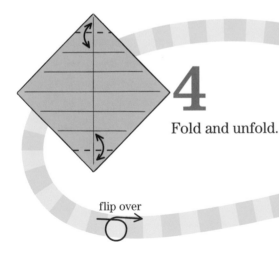

4 Fold and unfold.

flip over

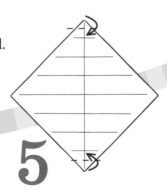

5 Fold tips to first crease.

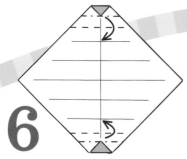

6

Pleat fold by making
a valley fold between
each mountain
crease.

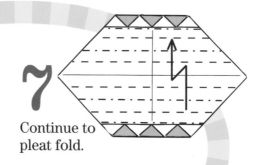

7

Continue to
pleat fold.

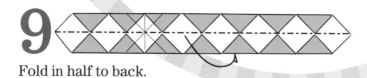

8

Fold and unfold
three times.

9

Fold in half to back.

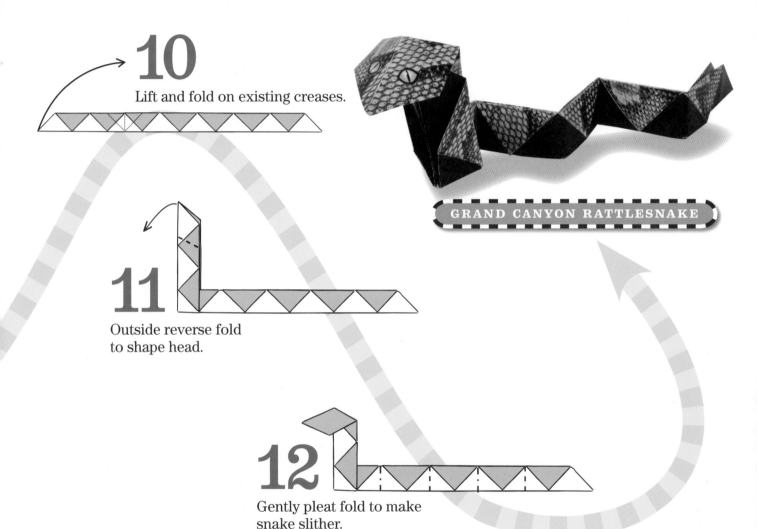

10
Lift and fold on existing creases.

11
Outside reverse fold to shape head.

12
Gently pleat fold to make snake slither.

GRAND CANYON RATTLESNAKE

Yellowstone's Big Horn Ram

I love camping! Camping is where everything is different. There is a real sense of adventure, seeing new things, and exploring the area around the campsite. The days are full of *"ings:"* hik*ing*, fish*ing*, swimm*ing*, explor*ing*, and all sorts other do*ings*. In the evening, everyone gathers around the campfire for a cookout, to play cards, and to tell stories. It's a simple time when kids and adults can enjoy just being together. Fold this Big Horn Ram to commemorate your hike to the top of a mountain, which is where the Big Horn Rams of Montana like to gather. Happy camp*ing*!

Yellowstone Junior Ranger

Are you between the ages of five and twelve? Want to become a Junior Ranger at the famous Yellowstone National Park? Participants discover interesting facts about the park's geology, wildlife, and weather. When you visit Yellowstone, make your first stop the Mammoth or Old Faithful Visitor Center to pick up your activity materials and supplies. Note to Mom and Dad: It costs only a few bucks to become a Junior Ranger. The kids get a nifty embroidered Junior Ranger patch upon completion and a review by a real National Park Ranger!

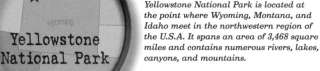

Yellowstone National Park

Yellowstone National Park is located at the point where Wyoming, Montana, and Idaho meet in the northwestern region of the U.S.A. It spans an area of 3,468 square miles and contains numerous rivers, lakes, canyons, and mountains.

How to Fold

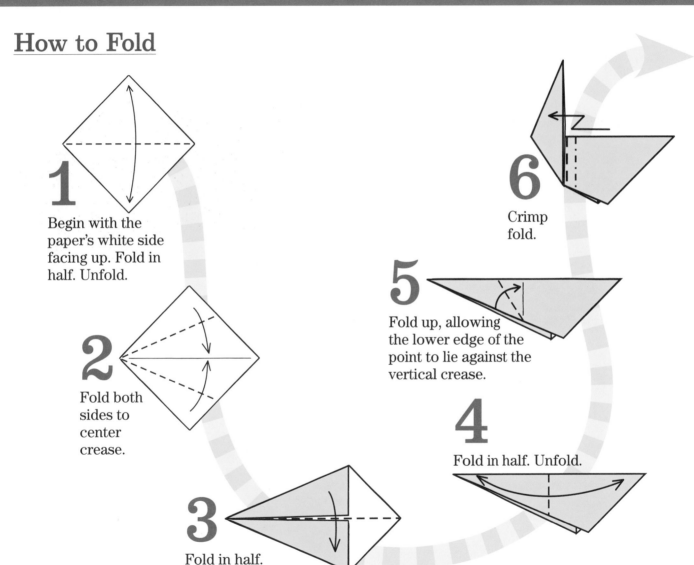

1 Begin with the paper's white side facing up. Fold in half. Unfold.

2 Fold both sides to center crease.

3 Fold in half.

4 Fold in half. Unfold.

5 Fold up, allowing the lower edge of the point to lie against the vertical crease.

6 Crimp fold.

Folding Yellowstone's Big Horn Ram

7

Fold top point to back so it lies along body. Fold top layer of bottom edge toward the inside so it is straight.

8

Fold top point back, but allow it to remain in front of body. Fold bottom back layer to match front.

YELLOWSTONE BIG HORN RAM

Model created by Marc Kirshenbaum

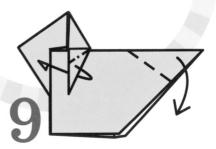

9

Fold to shape horn once more. Fold right side down to shape tail.

Nantucket Swordfish

NANTUCKET MASSACHUSETTS

If you spend the summer months in the deep waters off Nantucket Island, you might encounter the swashbuckler of the sea: the mighty swordfish. At 1,180 pounds and 15 feet long, this fish sure is a biggie. Legend has it that Ernest Hemingway was inspired to write *The Old Man and the Sea* by the story of a Nantucket fisherman who caught a swordfish that was bigger than his boat. Even though he was just a little boy when he heard it, Ernest knew a good fish tale when he heard one. That's the best thing about traveling: You hear the greatest stories!

Nantucket is an island 30 miles to the south of Cape Cod in Massachusetts, a state located in the New England region of the U.S.A.

Nantucket, Massachusetts

How to Fold

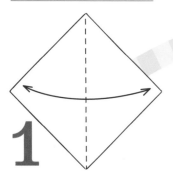

1 Begin with the paper's white side facing up. Fold in half. Unfold.

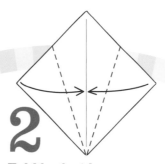

2 Fold both sides to center crease.

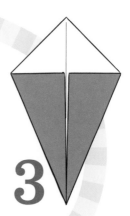

3

flip over

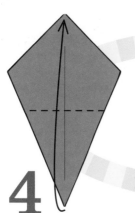

4 Fold lower tip to top edge.

flip over

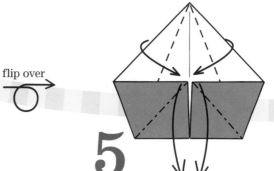

5 Open lower flaps and fold upper edges in at same time.

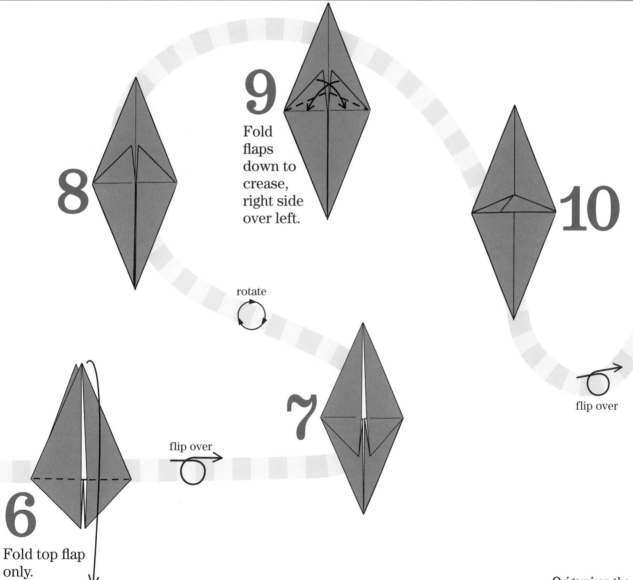

9 Fold flaps down to crease, right side over left.

8

10

rotate

flip over

7

flip over

6 Fold top flap only.

Folding the Nantucket Swordfish

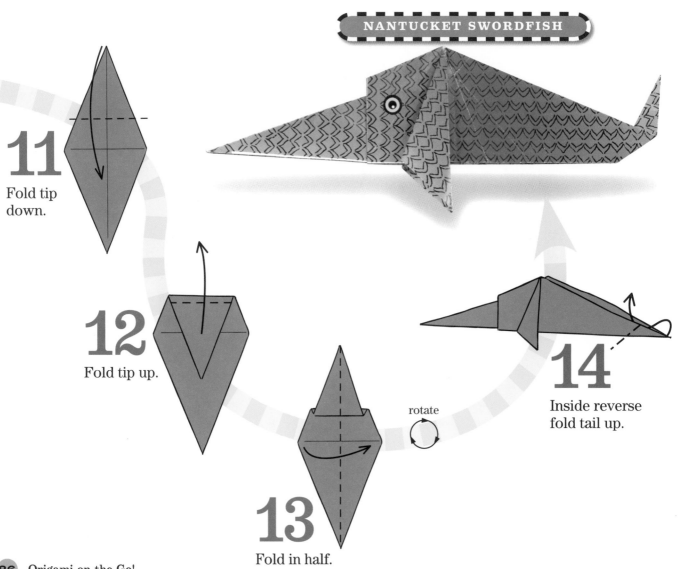

NANTUCKET SWORDFISH

11 Fold tip down.

12 Fold tip up.

13 Fold in half.

rotate

14 Inside reverse fold tail up.

African Elephant

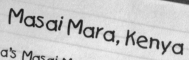

Weighing in at 12,000 pounds and standing more than twelve feet tall, the African elephant is the largest living land animal in the world. Twelve thousand pounds! How heavy is that? Let's calculate. If we divide the average weight of an elephant by something more familiar like, say, a Snickers bar, it would take approximately 96,000 bars to equal the weight of this massive creature!

Like an elephant, the instructions on the next pages are steady and sure-footed. Take it slow.

Masai Mara, Kenya

Africa's Masai Mara is the place to go for a safari. Imagine the enormous veldt, covered with tall golden grass and the occasional clump of trees. Herds of elephants, lions, gazelles, and buffalo are there. You can't miss the giraffes, hippopotamuses, antelopes, spotted hyenas, or the vultures circling above. Time your trip to coincide with the annual Great Migration, when thousands and thousands of zebras and wildebeests cross from Kenya's Masai Mara to the Serengeti in Tanzania. It's a scene you will never forget.

Masai Mara, Kenya

The Masai Mara is a park reserve in Kenya, a country in East Africa. The annual Great Migration occurs every year from July to October.

Folding the African Elephant

How to Fold

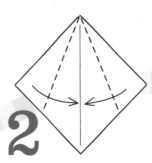

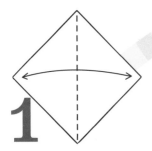

1 Begin with the paper's white side facing up. Fold and unfold.

2 Fold sides to center crease.

3 Fold tip to dot. Unfold.

4 Fold tip to dot. Unfold.

5 Unfold.

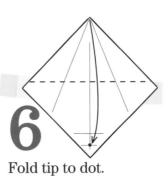

6 Fold tip to dot.

12

Slide to
the crease
line.
See next
step.

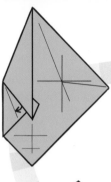

13

The top tip is bent upward. The model is
three-dimensional. Repeat Steps 11 and 12
on the right side.

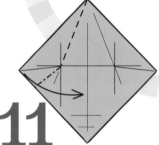

11

Fold to center, but do
not crease along the
mountain line.

10

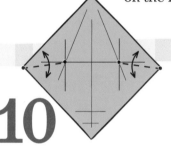

Fold and unfold.

9

Unfold
everything.

7

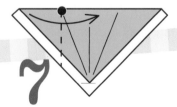

Left side folds
at crease to the right.

8

Note how creases line up at the
dot. Fold right side.

Folding the African Elephant

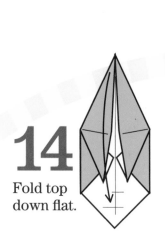

14 Fold top down flat.

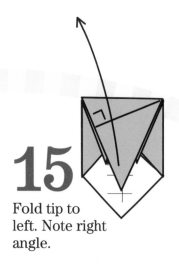

15 Fold tip to left. Note right angle.

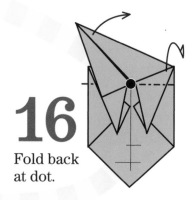

16 Fold back at dot.

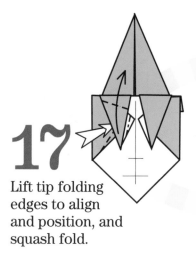

17 Lift tip folding edges to align and position, and squash fold.

18 The two lines with the dots are vertical, and the two angles are the same. Lift and squash fold.

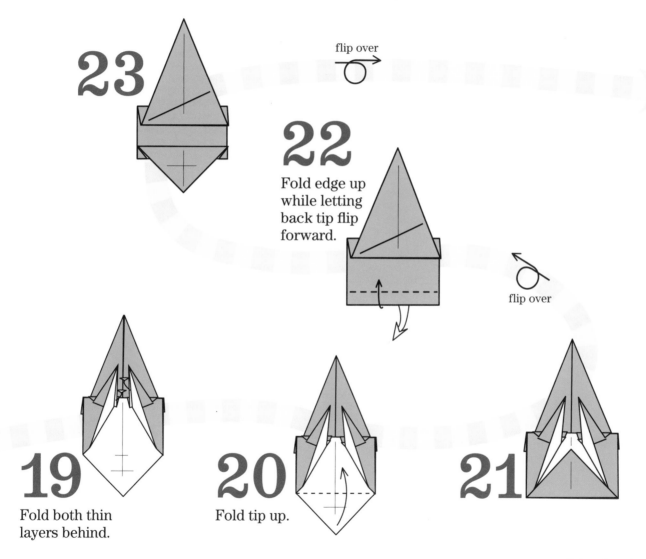

23

flip over

22

Fold edge up
while letting
back tip flip
forward.

flip over

19

Fold both thin
layers behind.

20

Fold tip up.

21

Folding the African Elephant

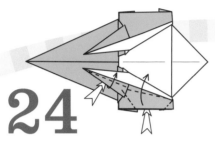

24 Together slowly fold tusk and legs back.

25 Repeat Step 24 on the top side.

Take it Slow

This mighty elephant has many details. Be patient—it's well worth it.

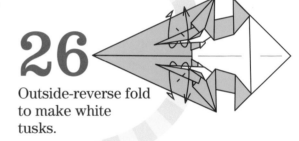

26 Outside-reverse fold to make white tusks.

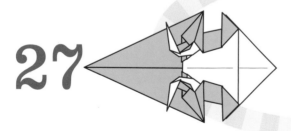

27

flip over

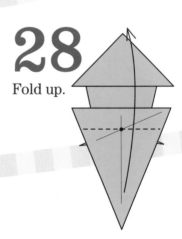

28 Fold up.

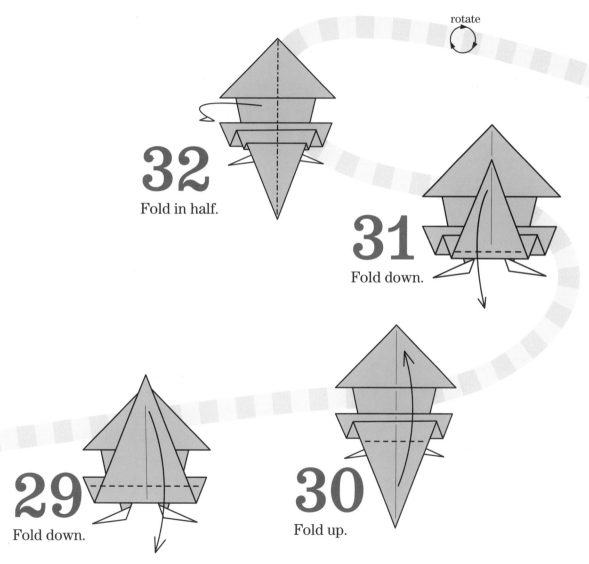

rotate

32

Fold in half.

31

Fold down.

29

Fold down.

30

Fold up.

Folding the African Elephant

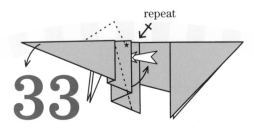

33

Slide the head and lower trunk while folding legs on both sides.

No Tears Tip

Gently hold head and pivot head up as trunk lowers.

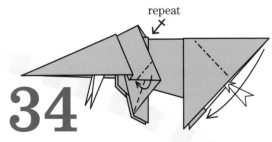

34

Fold ears on both sides and reverse fold the tail.

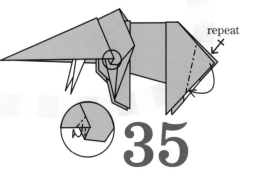

35

Fold in ears and reverse fold the tail. Repeat on other side.

36

Reverse fold the tusk. Fold inside at front leg, and reverse fold the tail. Repeat on other side.

37

Crimp fold the trunk, reverse fold the ear, and slowly fold the tail.

AFRICAN ELEPHANT

Model created by John Montroll

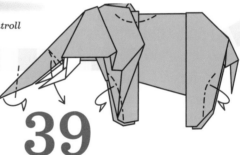

39

Shape trunk. Curve all legs. The lower part of the body will be slightly curved, too. Push in at the top.

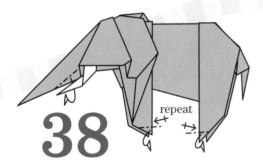

repeat

38

Shape tusk and feet. Repeat on other side.

German Nightingale

If you travel in the Harz Mountains in northern Germany, you may hear the sweet song of a nightingale. How will you identify the bird's alluring song? Nightingales are one of the few birds that sing after dark. So when you're walking back to your hotel after dinner, stop for a moment to listen to those sweet little birds whistling away in the dark forest. But don't go looking for them! Remember what happened to Hansel and Gretel? Beware, it is a *fact*: This region of Deutschland is full of witches.

Fairy-Tale Country

In the early nineteenth century, the brothers Wilhelm and Jakob Grimm had the wonderful idea to collect and preserve the ancient fairy tales of Europe. They invited townspeople from all over to share with them the tales told by their parents and grandparents, and wrote them down. "Little Red Riding Hood," "Snow White," "Sleeping Beauty," "The Pied Piper of Hamelin," and "Hansel and Gretel" are some of the more famous stories collected in *Grimm's Fairy Tales*. Read up on your fairy tales before you head to Germany so when a gnome asks you to guess his name, you can answer without hesitation:

RUMPELSTILTSKIN.

HARZ MOUNTAINS

GERMANY

The Harz Mountains are located in Germany, a country in central Europe. The word Harz is derived from the old German word Hardt, which means "mountain forest."

★ Harz Mountains, Germany

How to Fold

1 Begin with the paper's white side facing up. Fold in half.

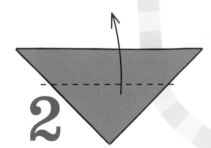

2 Fold top layer up.

3 Fold in half, right to left.

4 Fold top layer up.

rotate

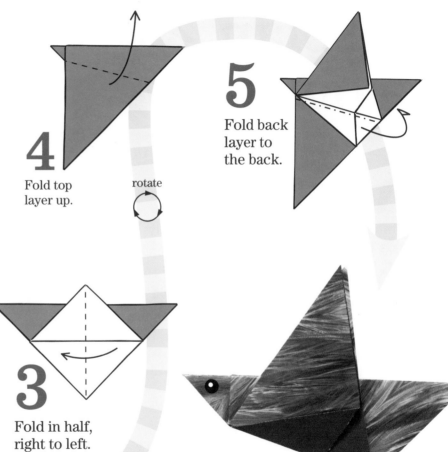

5 Fold back layer to the back.

GERMAN NIGHTINGALE

Russian Crow

With more than twenty-five distinct calls, crows are considered to be the world's most intelligent birds. Chatty and highly social, they live together in massively large groups called *murders*. You can find lots of crows throughout Russia. If you happen to see one, just ask it: А можно мне оди крекер? (A mozhno mne odin creker?) That's Russian for: "May I have a cracker, please?"

Siberia is a vast region in the northeast of Russia, which is the largest country in the world. Extending across northern Asia and almost half of Europe, Russia is 6,592,800 square miles big and spans eleven time zones.

Siberia, Russia

Out in Siberia

Think of the last time you went to a place with an enormous parking lot, like a zoo, a sports arena, or even a shopping mall. Perhaps, after parking the car, one of your parents said, "Oh my, we are parking out in Siberia!" As you took the long trek from the car to your destination, I'm sure you understood that the word *Siberia*, in this case, meant someplace "far away." The real Siberia is part of the Russian Federation and straddles the Arctic Circle. This enormous area is sparsely populated because of the harsh climate, long freezing-cold winters, and short wet summers. So the next time you face a long hike in a parking lot, be happy the parking space isn't really in Siberia.

How to Fold

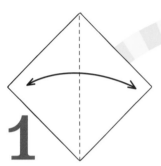

1 Begin with the paper's white side facing up. Fold in half. Unfold.

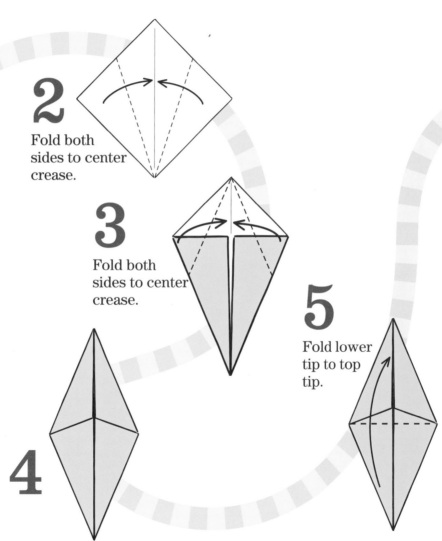

2 Fold both sides to center crease.

3 Fold both sides to center crease.

4

5 Fold lower tip to top tip.

Folding the Russian Crow

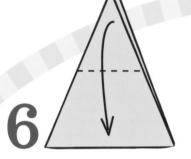

6 Fold top layer to bottom edge.

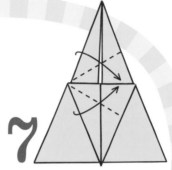

7 Fold both flaps to meet at center, then crease sharply.

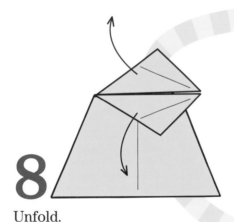

8 Unfold.

9 Fold both flaps to meet at center, then crease sharply.

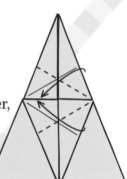

10

Unfold.

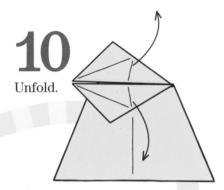

Caw! Caw! Caw!

RUSSIAN CROW

11

To shape body, fold lower flaps to back as head comes forward.

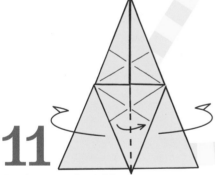

12

Hold lower edge of model and give it a flap back and forth.

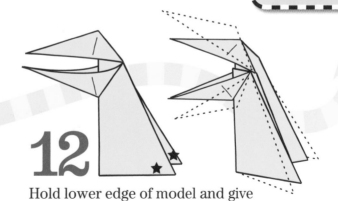

Greek Fish

T here's something magical about the Greek Isles. Something about the ultrablue sky and the turquoise seas, the white sand beaches, and the whitewashed houses that makes you feel like you've walked into a dream. No wonder the expression "halcyon days," meaning "calmness" or "tranquility," derives from an ancient Greek myth. It is said that the halcyon bird calmed the sea so it could build its nest on the surface of the water. Greece is the kind of place where you expect magical things like that to happen: birds building their nests on water, mermaids singing, and fish talking. Is that all true? It's Greek to me.

"Yassou!" Acropolis!

W hen you visit Greece, there is one place you should not miss: the collection of white marble temples called the Acropolis. Perched atop a rocky hillside overlooking the city of Athens, this dramatic complex will give you a glimpse of what the city looked like in the fifth century B.C.E. The ancient Greeks were extraordinary architects and master builders. How did they create these perfectly proportioned stone buildings without modern tools like laser levels, power saws, and forklifts? It is a true wonder!

When you see the Acropolis, don't forget to say "Yassou!" That means "hello" in Greek.

Athens is the largest city of Greece, as well as its capital. It is also one of the world's most ancient cities. Its recorded history goes back more than 3,000 years! Greece itself is located in southeastern Europe. It is comprised of a mainland and over 200 inhabited islands.

How to Fold

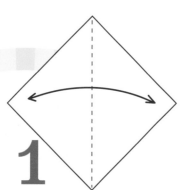

1 Begin with the paper's white side facing up. Fold in half. Unfold.

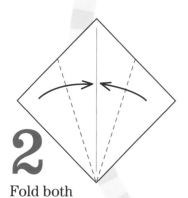

2 Fold both sides to center crease.

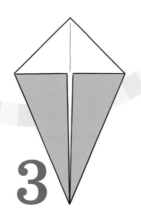

3

flip over

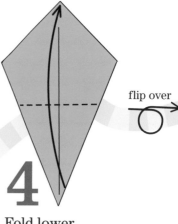

4 Fold lower tip to top tip.

flip over

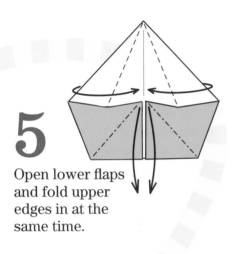

5 Open lower flaps and fold upper edges in at the same time.

GREEK FISH

6 Fold top tip outward. Repeat on other side.

repeat

rotate

7 Move tail to make fish talk.

NYC Pigeon

I n New York City, pigeons get a bad rap. After many hours pondering their habitat and habits, I have concluded these birds are obviously attracted to the best our culture has to offer. Look around any historic monument, significant building, or tourist hot spot in the city, and you will find a pigeon. They could easily fly away to a more natural setting, like Central Park, but these birds like to be in the thick of the bright city lights, crowds of people, and the thrill of urban life. Who is the first atop a hot restaurant or club? You guessed it: the pigeon! Now let's fold this discerning bird of high culture and good taste—Sir Pigeon.

New York City is located in the northeastern region of the United States. Home to the Statue of Liberty, the New York Stock Exchange, Rockefeller Center, and some of the tallest buildings in the world, including the Empire State Building, New York City consists of five boroughs: Manhattan, the Bronx, Brooklyn, Queens, and Staten Island.

NYC Pigeons Say "It's Hot"...

A ccording to the pigeons of New York City, here's a list of the top ten attractions you should check out next time you visit their city:

TIMES SQUARE: Day or night, it's always on. Pigeons love to gather under the bright lights.

THE BRONX ZOO: Where birds of many different feathers flock together.

MOMA (AKA MUSEUM OF MODERN ART): A favorite among artistic pigeons.

EMPIRE STATE BUILDING: Truly awesome and where romantic pigeons rendezvous.

THE AMERICAN MUSEUM OF NATURAL HISTORY: Birds are descended from dinosaurs, so of course pigeons love it here! You'll see flocks of pigeons on the steps in front of the museum.

SOUTH STREET SEAPORT: Not only is this place home to old sailing vessels you can visit, but it is also a venue for street performers.

LINCOLN CENTER: Home to the Metropolitan Opera, City Opera, American Ballet Theatre, and the New York Philharmonic. Pigeons love culture.

STATUE OF LIBERTY: A favorite among nesting pigeons.

GRAND CENTRAL TERMINAL: The grandest of transportation arrival and departure points. You can spot pigeons flying indoors sometimes.

ROCKEFELLER CENTER: Captains of industry call this place the office. Pigeons call it their favorite lunch spot.

Folding the NYC Pigeon

How to Fold

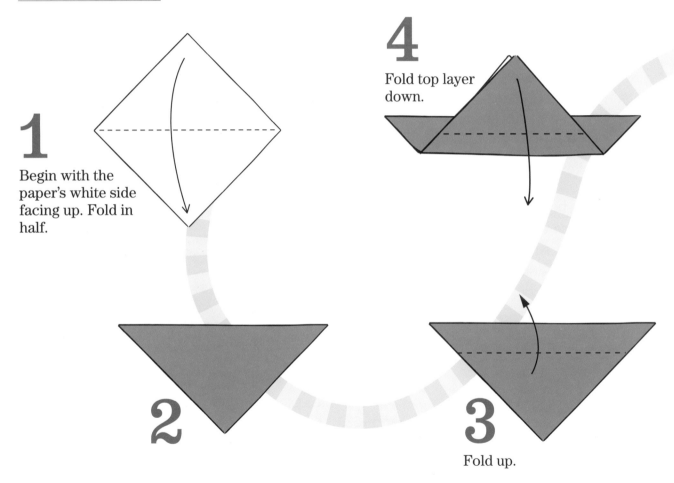

1 Begin with the paper's white side facing up. Fold in half.

2

3 Fold up.

4 Fold top layer down.

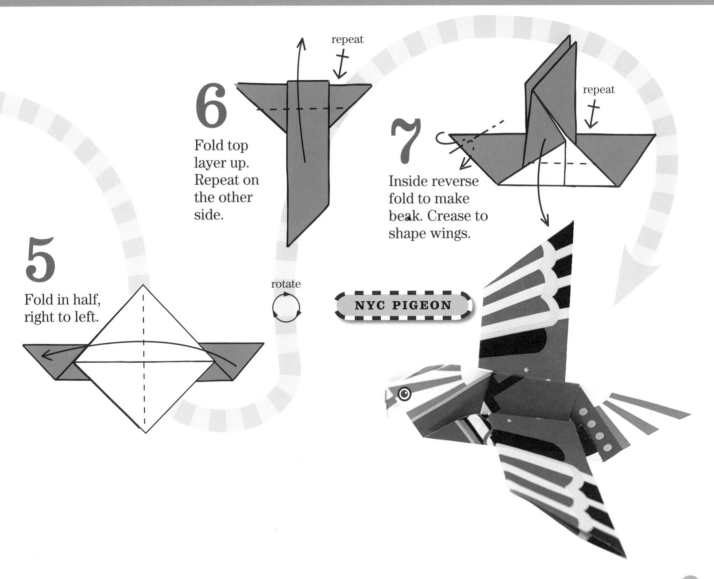

6 Fold top layer up. Repeat on the other side.

repeat

rotate

7 Inside reverse fold to make beak. Crease to shape wings.

repeat

5 Fold in half, right to left.

NYC PIGEON

Australian Koala Bear in a Tree

Upon arrival in southeastern Australia, take a deep breath. Do you smell something familiar? Can you guess what that is? No, it's not a cough drop factory over the hill. But you are getting warm . . . it is the natural aroma of the grand Eucalyptus tree. Not only people with sore throats crave the healing power of eucalyptus: It's also a favorite of Australia's fuzzy koala bear. These adorable, tree-hugging animals live on a diet of eucalyptus and gum leaves. They get water from the leaves, so they never have to leave the trees to wet their whistles. Paparazzi, beware: The koala is notoriously camera-shy! You may see only its paws as it hides behind a tree.

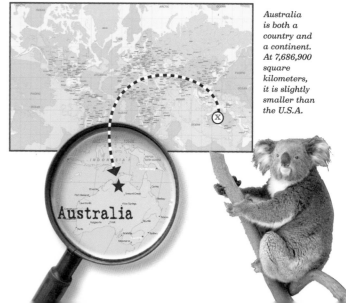

Australia is both a country and a continent. At 7,686,900 square kilometers, it is slightly smaller than the U.S.A.

Australia

How to Fold

You'll need three sheets of paper: one sheet for the tree trunk and two sheets of a different color for the bear.

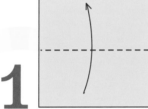

1 Begin with the paper's color side facing up. Fold in half.

repeat

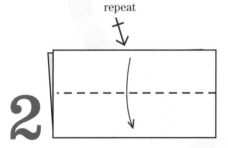

2 Fold top layer to bottom edge. Repeat on back.

3 Fold all layers toward middle of paper.

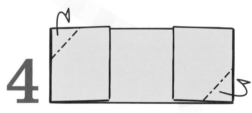

4 Fold corners to back.

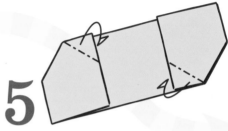

5 Fold corners behind.

6

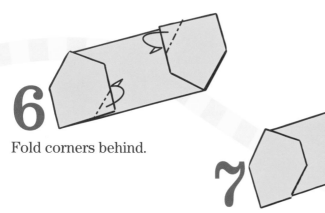

Fold corners behind.

7

Fold another set of paws,
repeating Steps 1 through 6.

8

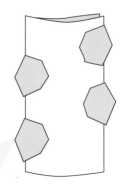

Wrap paws
around trunk.

AUSTRALIAN KOALA BEAR

How to Fold the Tree Trunk

1

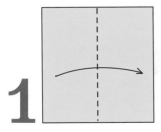

Begin with the paper's
color side facing up.
Fold in half.

2

Shape trunk by
curling sides back.

Model created by Nick Robinson

Agra Peacock

Agra·India

Nothing could be more exciting than planning a trip to exotic India. First stop: Agra, an ancient city located in northern India. Once the capital of the Mughul Empire, today this densely populated city is bustling with all sorts of adventure and amazing sights. See snake charmers and painted elephants, women dressed in jewel-colored saris and adorned with gold bangle bracelets, and entire families zooming by on scooters. No wonder the beautifully feathered peacock calls India home sweet home.

The Power Of Love

In the history of love stories, the one surrounding the Taj Mahal is arguably the best. The tale of a teenage crush that blossomed into romantic love will live on forever. Prince Shah Jahan first saw the love of his life in the palace bazaar when he was fifteen years old. It took five years before he wed his beautiful bride, Mumtaz Mahal. The prince became emperor, and he inherited magnificent wealth and power. Together, the couple had it all. Sadly, tragedy struck when Mumtaz Mahal died after giving birth to their fourteenth child. On her deathbed, Shah Jahan promised his wife that he would build her the most lavish mausoleum in the world. It took 20,000 craftsmen twenty years to complete the Taj Mahal.

India, a major country in South Asia, gets its name from the Indus River. The peacock is the national bird of India.

Folding the Agra Peacock

How to Fold

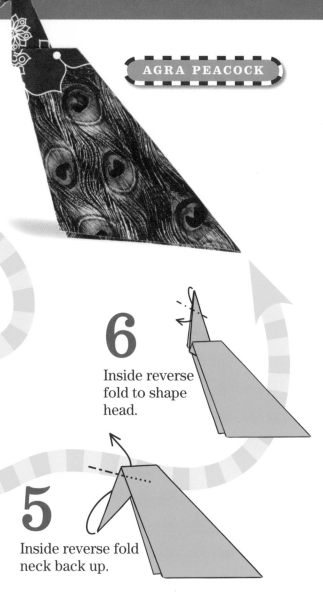

AGRA PEACOCK

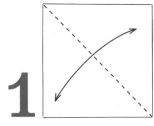

1 Begin with the paper's white side facing up. Fold in half. Unfold.

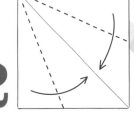

2 Fold left and right edges to center crease.

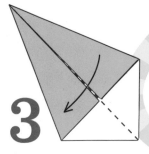

3 Fold in half.

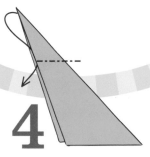

4 Inside reverse fold neck.

5 Inside reverse fold neck back up.

6 Inside reverse fold to shape head.

Zambia Giraffe

Imagine it's sunrise. You're heading out on your first safari–ever. The unspoiled landscape of Zambia's wildlife reserve leaves you breathless. In the near distance, you see a clump of trees and wonder: What is going on beyond those trees? Don't you wish you were tall enough to take a peek over the top of the branches? You may want to ask a giraffe what's happening. As the tallest animal on earth, the giraffe has a great view of all the action on the reserve. Even at birth, a baby giraffe is taller than the average man! And an adult male giraffe can grow as tall as 18 feet! How tall is 18 feet? you may wonder. Well, have three average-size men stand on top of one another and you'd get a good idea. Or better yet, run upstairs (or downstairs) to a second story window, because that's how high you'd have to be off the ground to pet the head of a giraffe. Nice view from up there, eh?

Victoria Falls

The massive Zambezi River cuts through the country of Zambia. Just before it crosses the border to Zimbabwe, it creates quite a stir. The locals call it Mosi-oa-Tunya (The Smoke that Thunders). We call it Victoria Falls. This waterfall is almost a mile wide when it pitches wildly over the edge and down into a gorge. Mosi-oa-Tunya creates a cloud of mist that can be seen from ten miles away. This sight is so spectacular that Victoria Falls is listed as one of the Seven Natural Wonders of the World.

Victoria Falls is so spectacular that it was named one of the Seven Natural Wonders of the world. What are the other six? The Grand Canyon in the U.S.A., the Great Barrier Reef in Australia, the harbor of Rio de Janeiro in Brazil, Mount Everest in Nepal, the Aurora Borealis (Northern Lights), and the Paricutin Volcano in Mexico.

Folding the Zambia Giraffe

How to Fold

To fold this model, you'll need two sheets of origami paper.

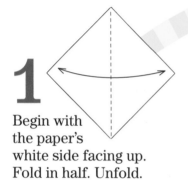

1 Begin with the paper's white side facing up. Fold in half. Unfold.

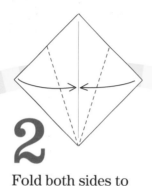

2 Fold both sides to center crease.

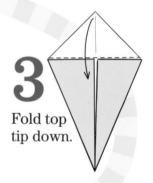

3 Fold top tip down.

4

flip over

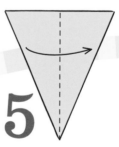

5 Fold in half.

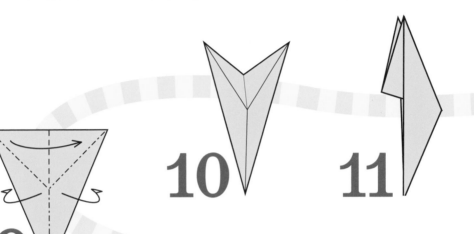

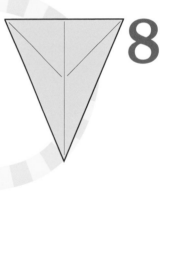

9

Fold on existing creases.

10

11

8

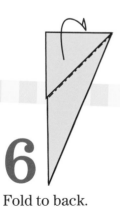

6

Fold to back.

7

Unfold and flatten.

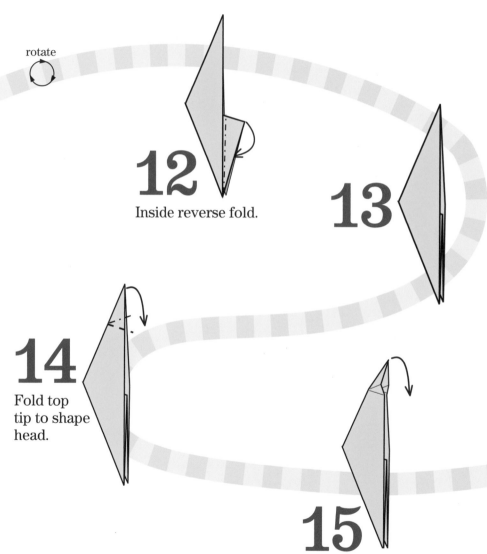

rotate

12
Inside reverse fold.

13

14
Fold top
tip to shape
head.

15

*Now, to fold the second unit:

flip over

19
Repeat steps 1-13 using second piece of paper. Flip over.

20
Inside reverse fold.

FIRST UNIT

18
Congratualtions! Your giraffe is halfway done.

repeat

cut

16
Cut small snip to make ears. Repeat on other side. Fold tip under.

17
Cut small snips to make mane.

Folding the Zambia Giraffe

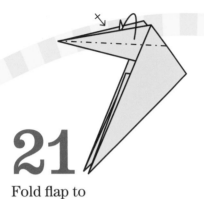

21
Fold flap to inside. Repeat on other side.

22
Outside reverse fold.

23
Fold tip of tail inside.

24

Add a drop of glue, or spot of glue stick.

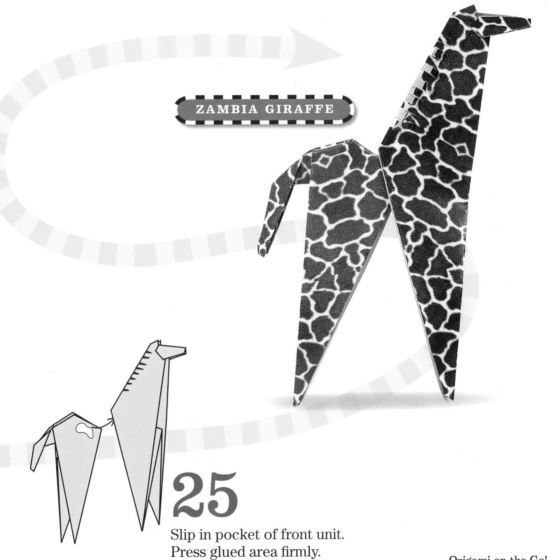

ZAMBIA GIRAFFE

25

Slip in pocket of front unit.
Press glued area firmly.

PART THREE

Cultural Treasures

The more you travel, the more you'll realize just how similar human beings are in all corners of the world. There are silly people, serious people, shy people, and outgoing people. There are helpful people and people who are not so helpful. There are boring people and exciting people. What makes them all different is their cultural background—the places, histories, and traditions that shape individual habits and character.

Chinese Opera Hat

Paper Trail

The history of papermaking and paper folding can be traced to first-century China and the Han Dynasty. The Chinese kept their paper skills top secret for some 500 years. It is not clear who let that cat out of the bag, but by the seventh century, the art of paper folding had made its way across the China Sea to Japan, where it was called "origami." The word is still in use today.

Classic Chinese opera is very different from Western opera. Chinese performers are trained not just in song, but in dance and acrobatics, too. Wearing elaborate costumes and colorful makeup, the performers put on quite a show. So why not join in the fun and fold this classic Chinese opera hat? Need a hat for your pet dog, cat, or bird? This jaunty little one-of-a-kind hat is sure to make you sing out with laughter!

Beijing, located in northern China, is the capital of the People's Republic of China. For over 800 years, Beijing has been the cultural center of China.

How to Fold

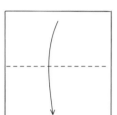

1 Begin with the paper's white side facing up. Fold in half.

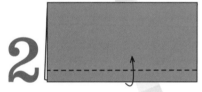

2 Fold top layer up about a half inch.

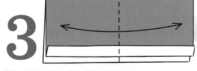

3 Fold in half. Unfold.

7 Open up to shape.

CHINESE OPERA HAT

6 Fold flap up.

5 Fold top flaps outward.

4 Fold left and right sides to center crease.

 flip over

British Royal Crown

It used to be that if you were sent to the Tower of London, your future looked grim indeed. The Tower was the most notorious prison in England. Today it houses the most valuable jewelry collection in the world: the British Crown Jewels. The collection includes gold scepters and swords, jeweled crowns, and rings encrusted with diamonds, rubies, emeralds, and pearls. Everyone loves a crown. Wearing a crown will turn a normal day into an extra special day. So don't wait for your next birthday to fold yourself a crown. A crown will turn any occasion into a royal affair.

I ♥ Pageantry

A pageant is a magnificent ceremonial event. People wear their finest clothes, shine up their brass buttons, and dust off their fanciest shoes for these events. Lucky for us, there is one country that still knows how to throw an event in the grandest of style, and that's England. When in London, be sure to see the Changing of the Guard at Buckingham Palace. The ceremony includes foot guards, sentries on horseback, and a military band attired in the most beautiful red coats with tall bearskin hats. The best part is, you don't have to be royalty to witness the splendor. The Changing of the Guard takes place every day in the summer months, and it is free for all people to enjoy.

London is the largest city in England and the United Kingdom. Founded more than 2,000 years ago by the Romans, it is a major tourist destination for travelers from all over the world.

How to Fold

Start with four sheets of letter-size paper

1

Fold paper in half. Unfold.

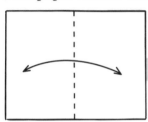

2

Fold to center crease. Unfold.

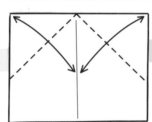

3

Fold top edges to creases.

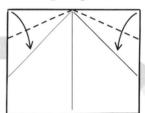

4

5

Fold on existing creases.

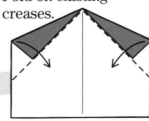

6

Fold bottom edge up.

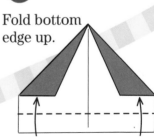

Folding the British Royal Crown

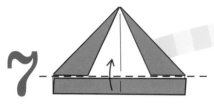

7 Fold bottom edge up, again.

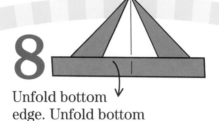

8 Unfold bottom edge. Unfold bottom edge, again.

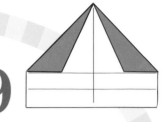

9 Fold three more units exactly the same.

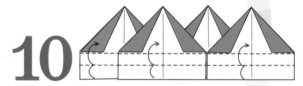

10 Overlay units as shown. Fold all bottom edges up at the same time.

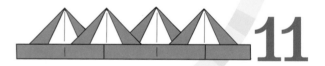

11

12 Slide each unit inside the other to lock.

BRITISH ROYAL CROWN

Model created by Laura Kruskal

Japanese Samurai Helmet

The mighty samurai warriors of Japan were honorable, loyal, moral, and humane. Famous for their elaborate armor and helmets, the noble samurai kept order all over the country for centuries. Follow the tradition of the samurai by folding this helmet slowly, precisely, and with honor.

Kyoto is a city in Japan that was the birthplace of the Samurai. It is located on the island of Honshu, one of the largest islands in Japan, which is an archipelago comprised of over 3,000 islands.

Folding the Japanese Samurai Helmet

How to Fold

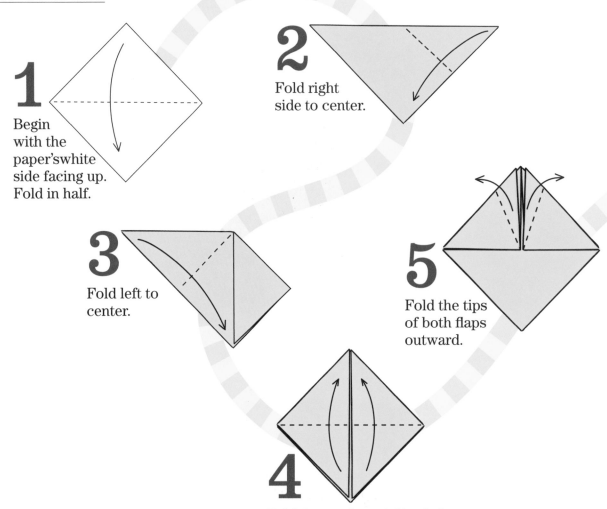

1 Begin with the paper's white side facing up. Fold in half.

2 Fold right side to center.

3 Fold left to center.

4 Fold the top layer of both flaps up.

5 Fold the tips of both flaps outward.

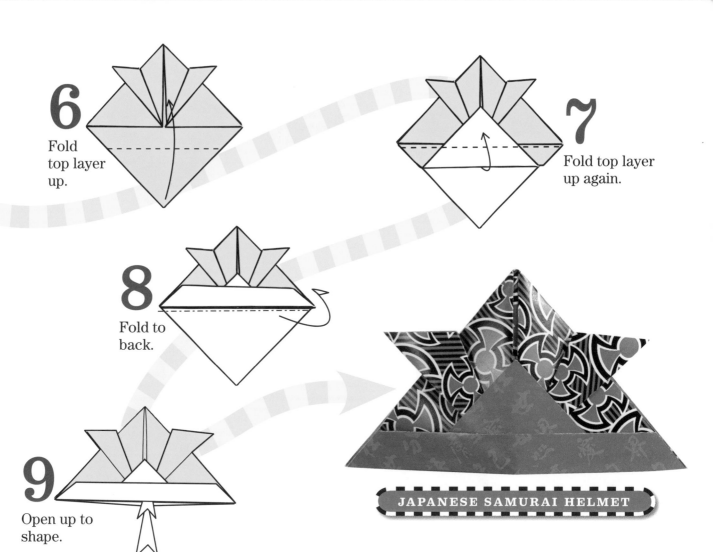

6 Fold top layer up.

7 Fold top layer up again.

8 Fold to back.

9 Open up to shape.

JAPANESE SAMURAI HELMET

Canadian Canoe

There is more fresh water covering parts of the surface of Canada than any other country of the world. Canada has some 31,754 bodies of water (204 of which are named Long Lake, 182 are called Mud Lake, and 100 go by Moose Lake). Given these numbers, what better way to see the beauty of this country than by exploring its waterways by canoe? You will be amazed at all the details you will see and hear while gliding across the water. Try this: No talking for five minutes. Just take in all the sights and sounds of nature, the feeding birds, the wind in the trees, and the currents moving through the water. Cutting down on noise pollution is an environmentally friendly way to travel.

Lakes So Great We Share Them

Along the border between Canada and the United States stretches a chain of five magnificent lakes: Lake Superior, Lake Michigan, Lake Huron, Lake Erie, and Lake Ontario. These lakes contain one fifth of the world's entire fresh surface water. How much water is that? Picture this: If you drained all the water out of all the Great Lakes and spilled it out over the land instead, it would cover the contiguous United States (that's from California to Maine and all the states in between) with ten feet of water.

Great Lakes

The Great Lakes are located in the eastern region of North America. They are bounded by Ontario on the Canadian side and Minnesota, Wisconsin, Ohio, Illinois, Indiana, Michigan, Pennsylvania, and New York on the U.S. side.

How to Fold

1

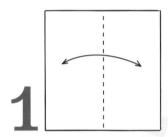

Begin with the paper's white side facing up. Fold in half. Unfold.

2

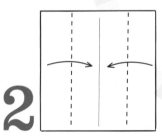

Fold to center crease.

3

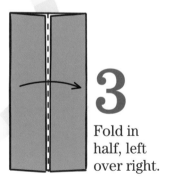

Fold in half, left over right.

4

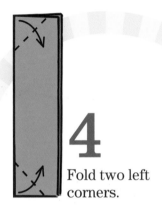

Fold two left corners.

5

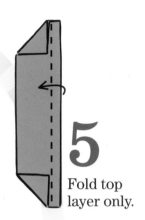

Fold top layer only.

Folding the Canadian Canoe

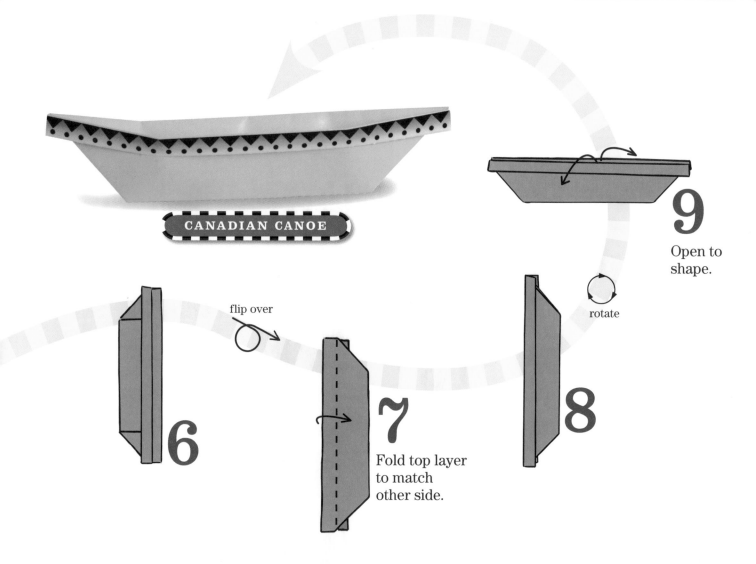

CANADIAN CANOE

9 Open to shape.

rotate

flip over

6

7 Fold top layer to match other side.

8

Egyptian Mummy

The mysteries of Ancient Egypt have fascinated people for thousands of years. The temples and tombs were decorated inside and out with beautiful paintings and magical hieroglyphs. Ancient Egyptians believed in the renewal of life beyond the grave. Don't be frightened, though: Mummies don't rise up from the dead. Egyptians believed their *ka*, or soul, would rise to the heavens and live an eternal life. What do curious minds want to know? Is there really a preserved body under all the linen wrappings? The answer is *Yes.*

Cairo is the capital city of Egypt, a country located in North Africa. Situated on the banks of the Nile River, Cairo is home to the pyramids and Great Sphinx of Giza, as well as the Egyptian Museum, which contains the largest collection of ancient Egyptian antiquities in the world—including the mummies of King Tut and other Egyptian kings.

Cairo, Egypt

Curse of The Mummy

Leave it to reporters to come up with the wacky "Curse of the Mummy" story. It all started in 1923, when English archaeologist Howard Carter discovered the sealed tomb of King Tutankhamun, an Egyptian pharoah who ruled Egypt over 3,300 years ago. The public was fascinated with the discovery and the story was selling newspapers like mad (remember, this is long before television news or the Internet). Mr. Carter's benefactor, Lord Carnarvon (who financed the expedition), got an infection and died shortly after the tomb was opened. After that, every reporter added a little extra drama to the tragedy. Thus the story of the "curse" was born—and even *more* newspapers were sold!

How to Fold

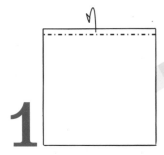

1 Begin with white paper. Fold top edge to back.

2 Fold top edge forward.

3

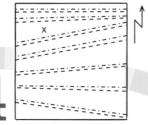

4 Continue to fold more thin pleats. Leave gap for neck at ×.

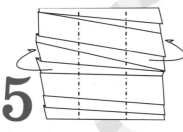

5 Fold sides to back.

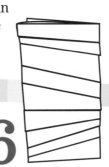

6

flip over

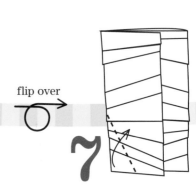

7 Fold up lower corner.

flip over

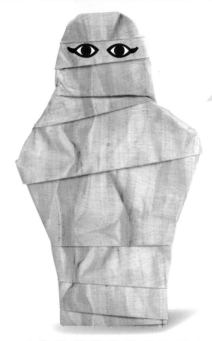

EGYPTIAN MUMMY

Model created by Anita Barbour

11

Shape shoulders and head.

10

Pleat fold to shape neck.

8

To shape curved edge, slowly tug in opposite directions. Repeat Steps 7 and 8 on right side.

9

Fold top corners, to shape curved shoulders as in Step 5.

Hollywood Star

Starstruck in La-La Land (aka Los Angeles)? Check out the courtyard at Grauman's Chinese Theater in Hollywood where you can literally touch the hand—well, the handprint—of some of your favorite movie stars. Give a high five to the stars of the *Harry Potter* films Daniel Radcliffe (Harry), Rupert Grint (Ron), and Emma Watson (Hermione). Next, check out Hollywood's Walk of Fame on Hollywood Boulevard (from Gower to La Brea) to see the stars lining the sidewalk. Be sure to eat a hearty breakfast, because you'll need to muster all your star power to walk past the more than 2,000 granite stars.

Now you, too, can be a star. Follow the simple folding instruction to make the perfect five-point star for your dressing (or hotel) room door.

Location, Location, Location

It is true: Location makes all the difference. Back in the 1910s, when filmmakers were looking for the perfect spot to shoot their films, they gravitated toward southern California. They were attracted by the mild climate and the fabulous sunlight, which makes it possible to film outdoors year-round. In Los Angeles, the sky is clear an average 187 days a year. Get Ready. Set. And Action!

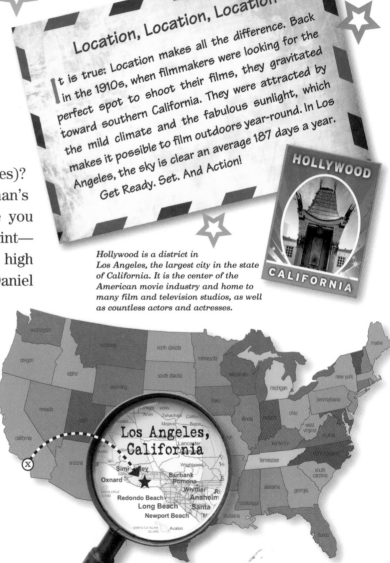

Hollywood is a district in Los Angeles, the largest city in the state of California. It is the center of the American movie industry and home to many film and television studios, as well as countless actors and actresses.

How to Fold

To fold this model, you'll need two sheets of origami paper.

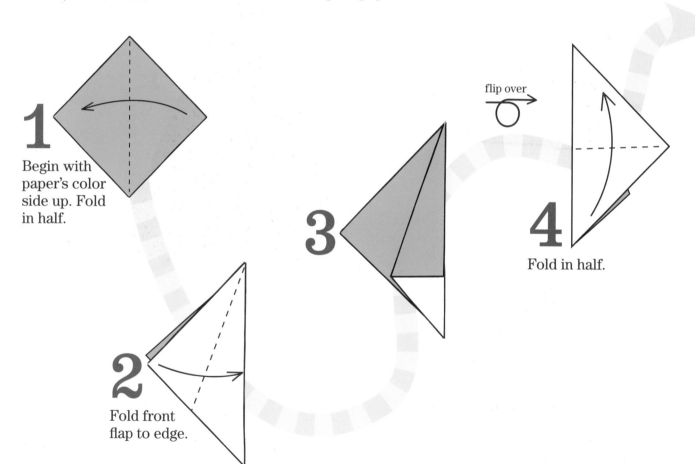

1 Begin with paper's color side up. Fold in half.

2 Fold front flap to edge.

3

flip over

4 Fold in half.

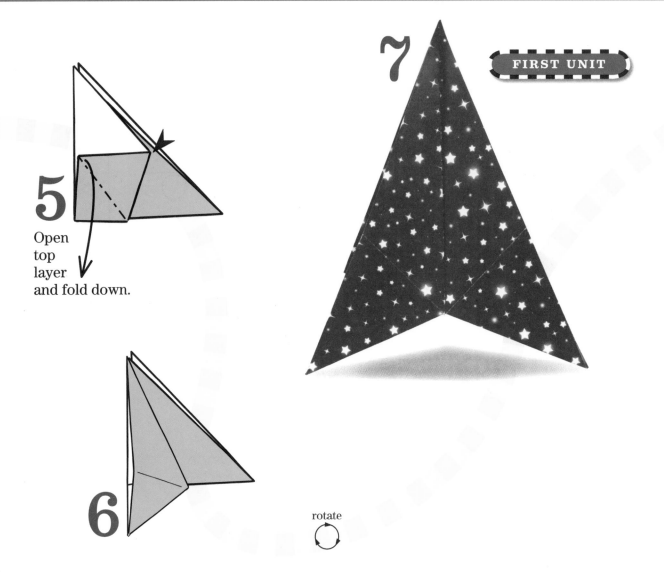

5 Open top layer and fold down.

6

7

FIRST UNIT

rotate

*Now, to fold the second unit:

HOLLYWOOD STAR

8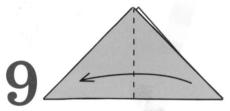

Begin with the paper's white side facing up. Fold in half.

9

Fold in half.

10

Add a drop of glue, or spot of glue stick.

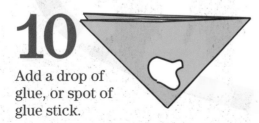

11

Slip triangle between layers of first unit.

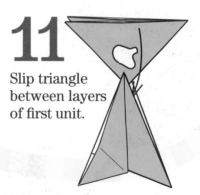

home sweet home

PART FOUR

The Voyage Home

Ready to pack it up and head home? During the journey, you'll be thinking about all the exciting stories you'll share with your friends. Like the day when you all got lost but then found the most amazing lake and went swimming, or when you saw a real snake charmer in Delhi with a real cobra in a real basket! Really!

The most surprising thing is that later, when the car pulls into your driveway or you open the front door to your apartment, you'll be happy to be back home. You'll be happy to sleep in your own bed, eat your normal breakfast, and walk down those familiar streets again, because it is so true: There is no place like home.

Gift Box

Make a gift box to transport your travel treasures back home safely. How about decorating it with a theme from your travels, adding color, texture, or spelling out the name of the place you visited in decorative lettering. Cut a postcard to fit into the bottom of the box for added durability. Any way you choose to decorate it, this gift box will surely make a great souvenir. Make a pair of boxes, a top and a bottom, and you are set to carry your treasures.

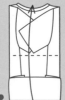

Refolding Your Gear

Why do dirty clothes seem to take up so much more room than clean ones? Well, I think we can thank the expert folding skills of our laundress (thank you, Mom). At the end of your trip, when you are ready to pack your bag to travel home, it is time to put your origami folding skills to work. Follow the folding instructions to refold all your shirts into a uniform stack to maximize every cubic inch of your bag.

HOW TO FOLD A T-SHIRT

1. Lay T-shirt down and smooth it out. Flip over.

2. Fold sides toward center, overlapping sleeves. Smooth flat.

3. Fold bottom edge up. This fold is key.

4. Fold bottom edge to meet neck band. Flip over.

5.

How to Fold

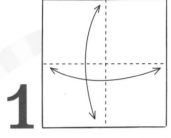

1 Begin with the paper's white side facing up. Fold and unfold in both directions.

rotate

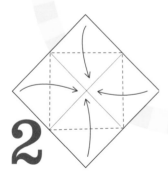

2 Fold corners to center.

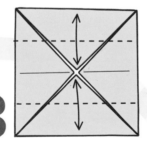

3 Fold top and bottom edge to meet at center crease. Unfold.

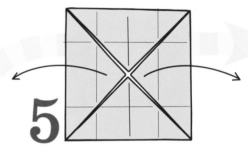

4 Fold right and left edges to meet at center crease. Unfold.

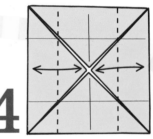

5 Unfold right and left flap only.

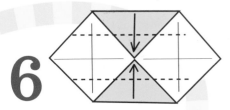

6

Fold top and bottom edge to meet at center crease.

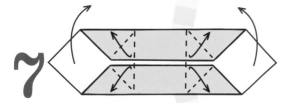

7

Shape box by lifting as you fold, one corner at a time.

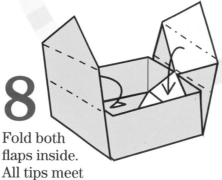

8

Fold both flaps inside. All tips meet in center of box.

GIFT BOX

Travel Frame

Fold this swanky little travel frame for your favorite memory of the trip. It could be a picture of you riding a painted elephant in India or a wacky camel in Egypt, or a photograph of your cousin on the North Rim of the Grand Canyon, or that funny snapshot of your grandmother holding up the huge fish she caught. Whichever image you choose, it will be one moment of many from your fabulous adventures away from home. When selecting a piece of paper for the frame, be sure to think about which color will best complement your photograph.

Agra, India

Canada

Oahu, Hawaii

Folding the Travel Frame

How to Fold

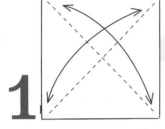

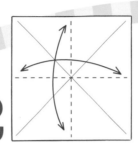

1 Begin with the paper's white side facing up. Fold and unfold in both directions.

2 Fold and unfold in both directions.

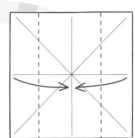

3 Fold right and left edges to meet at center crease.

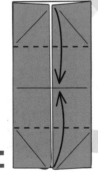

4 Fold top and bottom edges to meet at center crease.

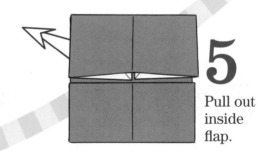

5 Pull out inside flap.

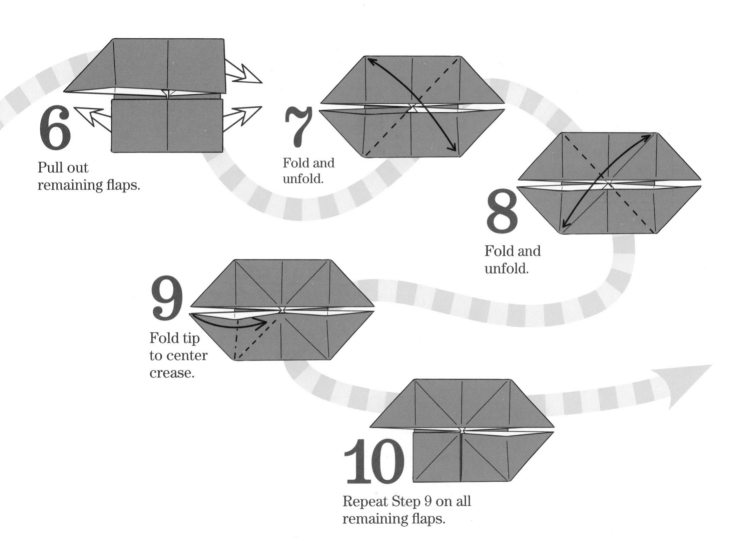

6 Pull out remaining flaps.

7 Fold and unfold.

8 Fold and unfold.

9 Fold tip to center crease.

10 Repeat Step 9 on all remaining flaps.

Folding the Travel Frame

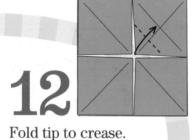

11
Fold tip to corner and unfold.

12
Fold tip to crease.

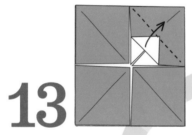

13
Fold over on existing crease.

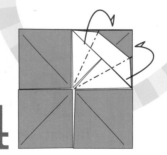

14
Fold both sides to back.

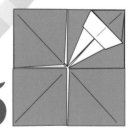

15
Repeat Steps 11 through 14 on remaining corners.

16

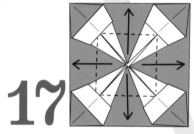

17

Fold corner tips to
outside edges.

TRAVEL FRAME

18 photo

Size photograph
larger than the
opening.

19

Insert photograph
into pocket.

MAP OF THE WORLD

Use this map of the world—and the handy travel stickers on the next few pages—to help you keep track of your travels. Now you'll always know where you're going, and remember where you've been.

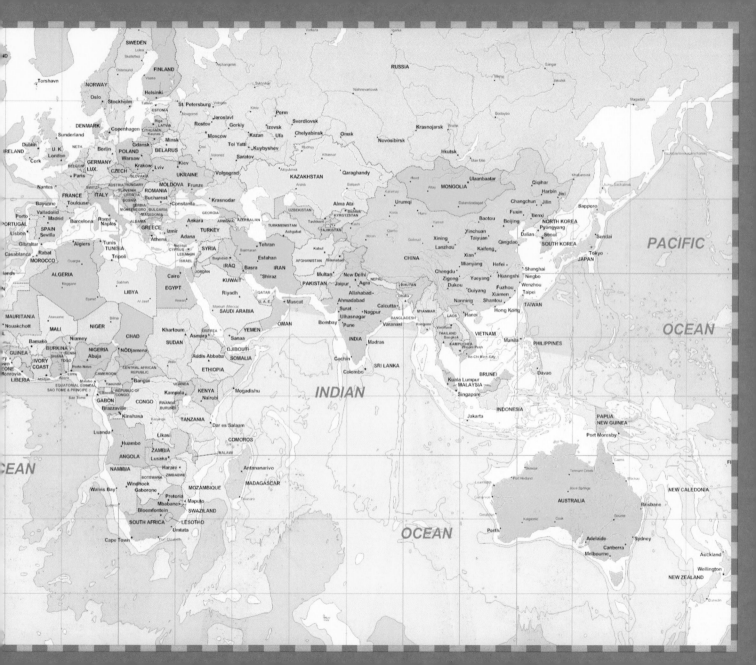

During the next few months, don't be surprised if you get bitten by the traveling bug again. It gets you when you least expect it: riding your bike, watching a movie, or shampooing your hair. In a flash, wanderlust will take hold of you. Just get out Origami on the Go!, fold a model, and start dreaming of another adventure.

Bon Voyage.

Margaret Van Sicklen

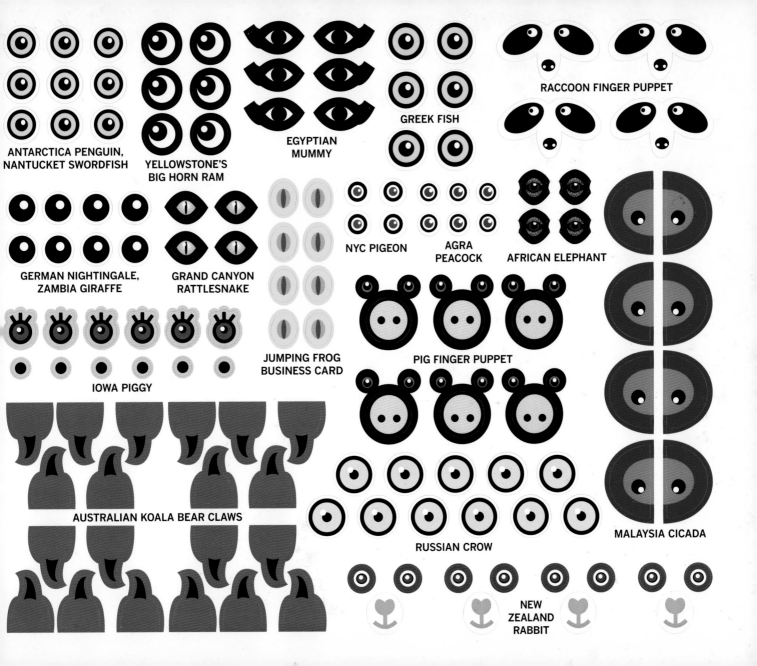

ANTARCTICA PENGUIN, NANTUCKET SWORDFISH

YELLOWSTONE'S BIG HORN RAM

EGYPTIAN MUMMY

GREEK FISH

RACCOON FINGER PUPPET

GERMAN NIGHTINGALE, ZAMBIA GIRAFFE

GRAND CANYON RATTLESNAKE

NYC PIGEON

AGRA PEACOCK

AFRICAN ELEPHANT

IOWA PIGGY

JUMPING FROG BUSINESS CARD

PIG FINGER PUPPET

AUSTRALIAN KOALA BEAR CLAWS

RUSSIAN CROW

MALAYSIA CICADA

NEW ZEALAND RABBIT

SNAIL MAIL ENVELOPE

TO:_____
_____
_____

TO:_____
_____
_____

TO:_____
_____
_____

BRITISH
ROYAL
CROWN

I WANT TO GO HERE   I WANT TO GO HERE   I WANT TO GO HERE   I WANT TO GO HERE   I WANT TO GO HERE   I WANT TO GO HERE   I WANT TO GO HERE

BERLIN
GERMANY

MOUNT EVEREST
HIMALAYAS

NANTUCKET
MASSACHUSETTS

KENYA
AFRICA

STRATFORD-UPON-AVON
SHAKESPEARE
ENGLAND

HOLLYWOOD
CALIFORNIA

Agra·India

ZAMBIA
AFRICA

LONDON
ENGLAND

TREVI FOUNTAIN ROME
ITALY

GREAT LAKES
USA · CANADA

DES MOINES
IOWA

ATHENS
GREECE

Southern Ocean
ANTARCTICA

PAHANG
MALAYSIA

KYOTO
JAPAN

CAIRO · EGYPT

LOUISIANA
U·S·A

BEIJING
CHINA

GRAND CANYON
ARIZONA · USA

"Green" Fan (page 4)

"Green" Fan (page 4)

"Green" Fan (page 4)

"Green" Fan (page 4)

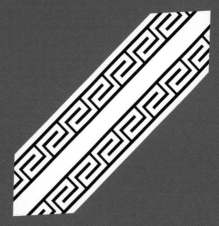

WE ARE HAPPY
TO SERVE
YOU

WE ARE HAPPY
TO SERVE
YOU

WE ARE HAPPY
TO SERVE
YOU

"Cheers!" Paper Cup (page 6)

"Cheers!" Paper Cup (page 6)

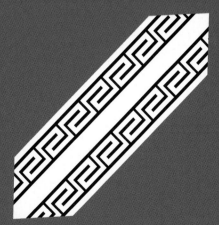

WE ARE HAPPY
TO SERVE
YOU

WE ARE HAPPY
TO SERVE
YOU

"Cheers!" Paper Cup (page 6)

Stunt Plane (page 14)

Stunt Plane (page 14)

Stunt Plane (page 14)

Stunt Plane (page 14)

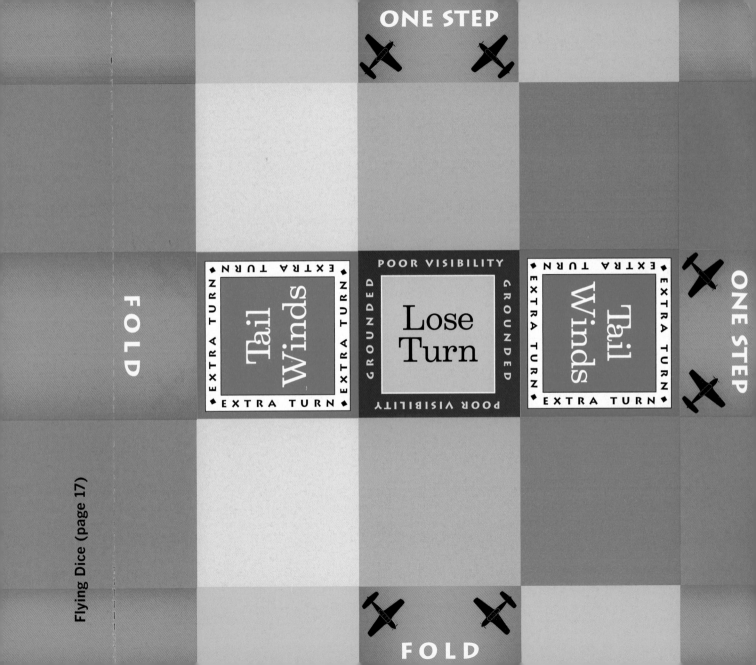

ONE STEP

FOLD

ONE STEP

Flying Dice (page 17)

EXTRA TURN • EXTRA TURN
Tail Winds
EXTRA TURN • EXTRA TURN

POOR VISIBILITY
GROUNDED
Lose Turn
GROUNDED
POOR VISIBILITY

EXTRA TURN • EXTRA TURN
Tail Winds
EXTRA TURN • EXTRA TURN

FOLD

Flying Dice (page 17)

ONE STEP

FOLD

Flying Dice (page 17)

EXTRA TURN • EXTRA TURN
Tail Winds
EXTRA TURN • EXTRA TURN

POOR VISIBILITY
GROUNDED
Lose Turn
GROUNDED
POOR VISIBILITY

EXTRA TURN • EXTRA TURN
Tail Winds
EXTRA TURN • EXTRA TURN

ONE STEP

FOLD

Flying Dice (page 17)

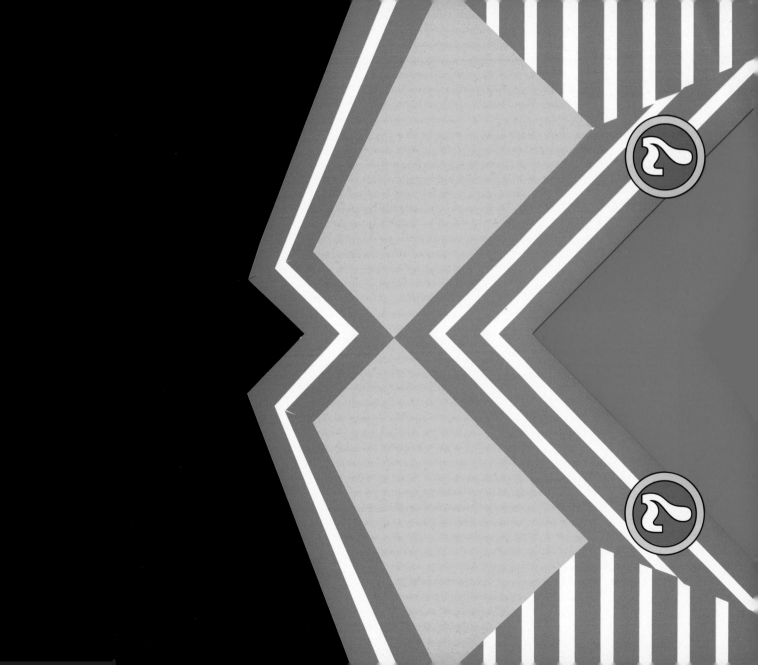

Lucky 7 Plane (page 21)

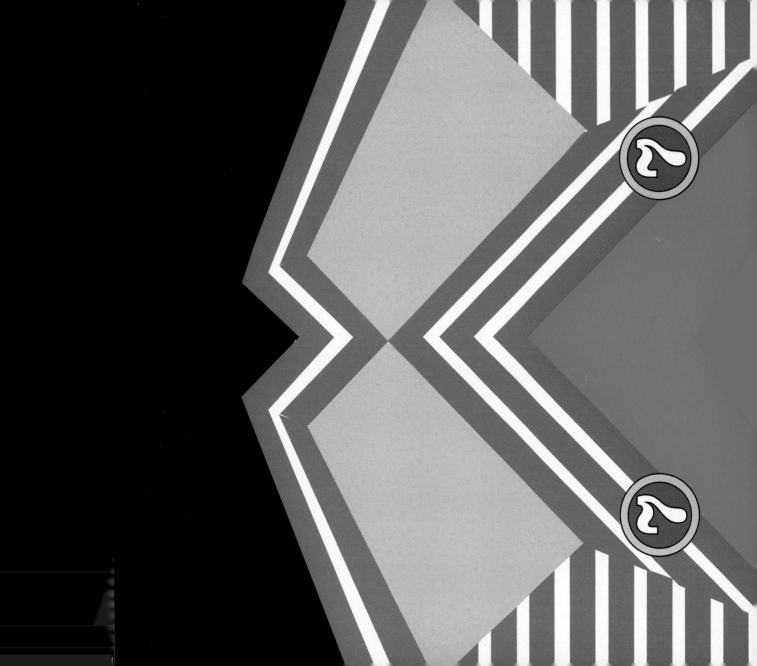

Lucky Seven Plane (page 21)

Raccoon Finger Puppet (page 33)

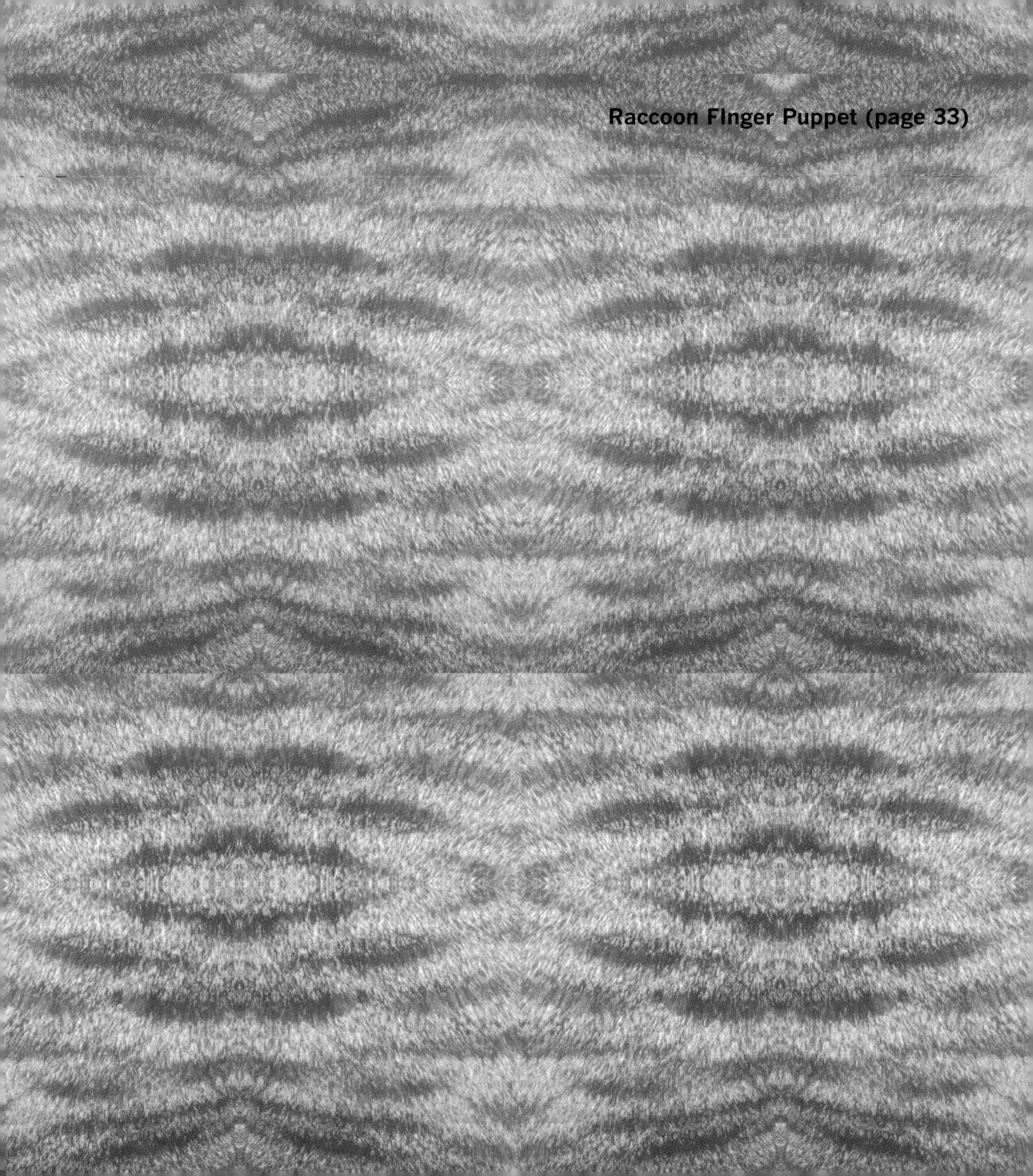

Raccoon Finger Puppet (page 33)

Raccoon Finger Puppet (page 33)

Pig Finger Puppet (page 37)

Pig Finger Puppet (page 37)

Fortune Teller (page 41)

Fortune Teller (page 41)

Fortune Teller (page 41)

Fortune Teller (page 41)

Knick-knack Box (page 47)

Knick-knack Box (page 47)

Knick-knack Box (page 47)

Knick-knack Box (page 47)

Heart Place Card (page 54)

Heart Place Card (page 54)

Heart Place Card (page 54)

Heart Place Card (page 54)

Iowa Piggy (page 60)

Iowa Piggy (page 60)

Iowa Piggy (page 60)

Iowa Piggy (page 60)

Malaysia Cicada (page 63)

Malaysia Cicada (page 63)

Malaysia Cicada (page 63)

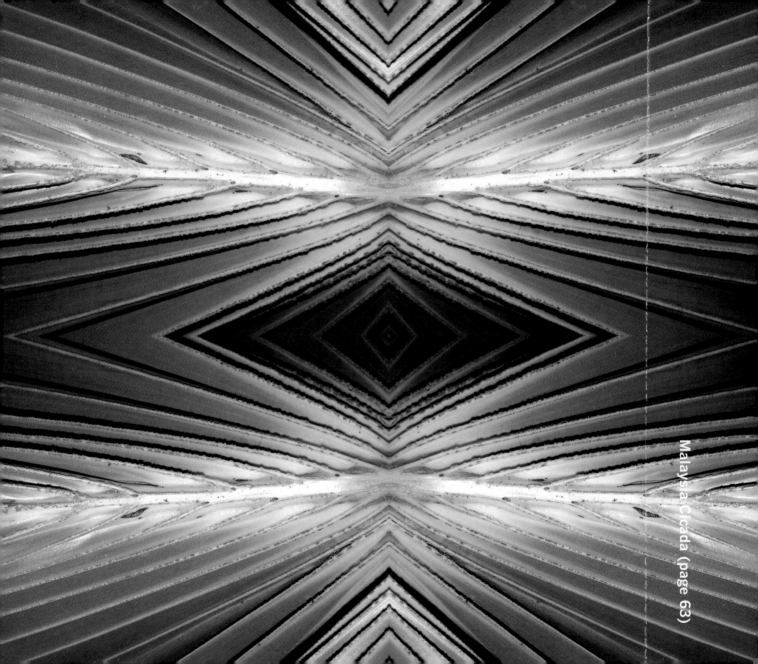

Malaysia Cicada (page 63)

New Zealand Rabbit (page 66)

New Zealand Rabbit (page 66)

New Zealand Rabbit (page 66)

New Zealand Rabbit (page 66)

Amazon River Turtle (page 70)

Amazon River Turtle (page 70)

Amazon River Turtle (page 70)

Amazon River Turtle (page 70)

Antarctica Penguin (page 73)

Antarctica Penguin (page 73)

Antarctica Penguin (page 73)

Antarctica Penguin (page 73)

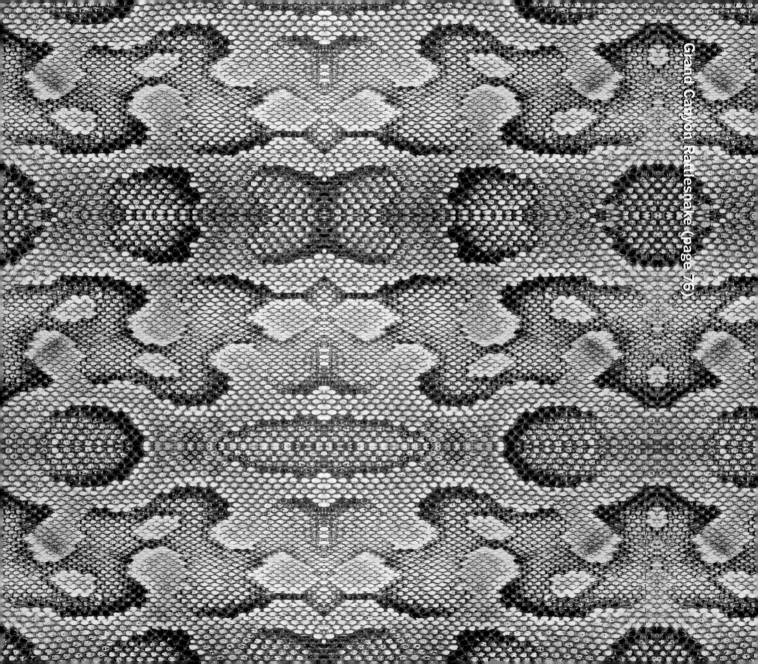

Grand Canyon Rattlesnake (page 76)

Grand Canyon Rattlesnake (page 76)

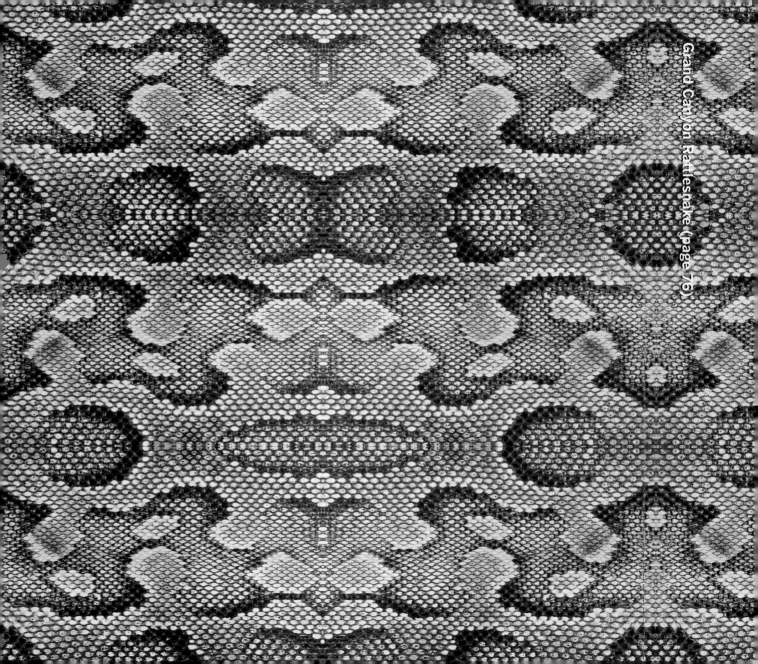

Grand Canyon Rattlesnake (page 76)

Yellowstone's Big Horn Ram (page 80)

Nantucket Swordfish (page 83)

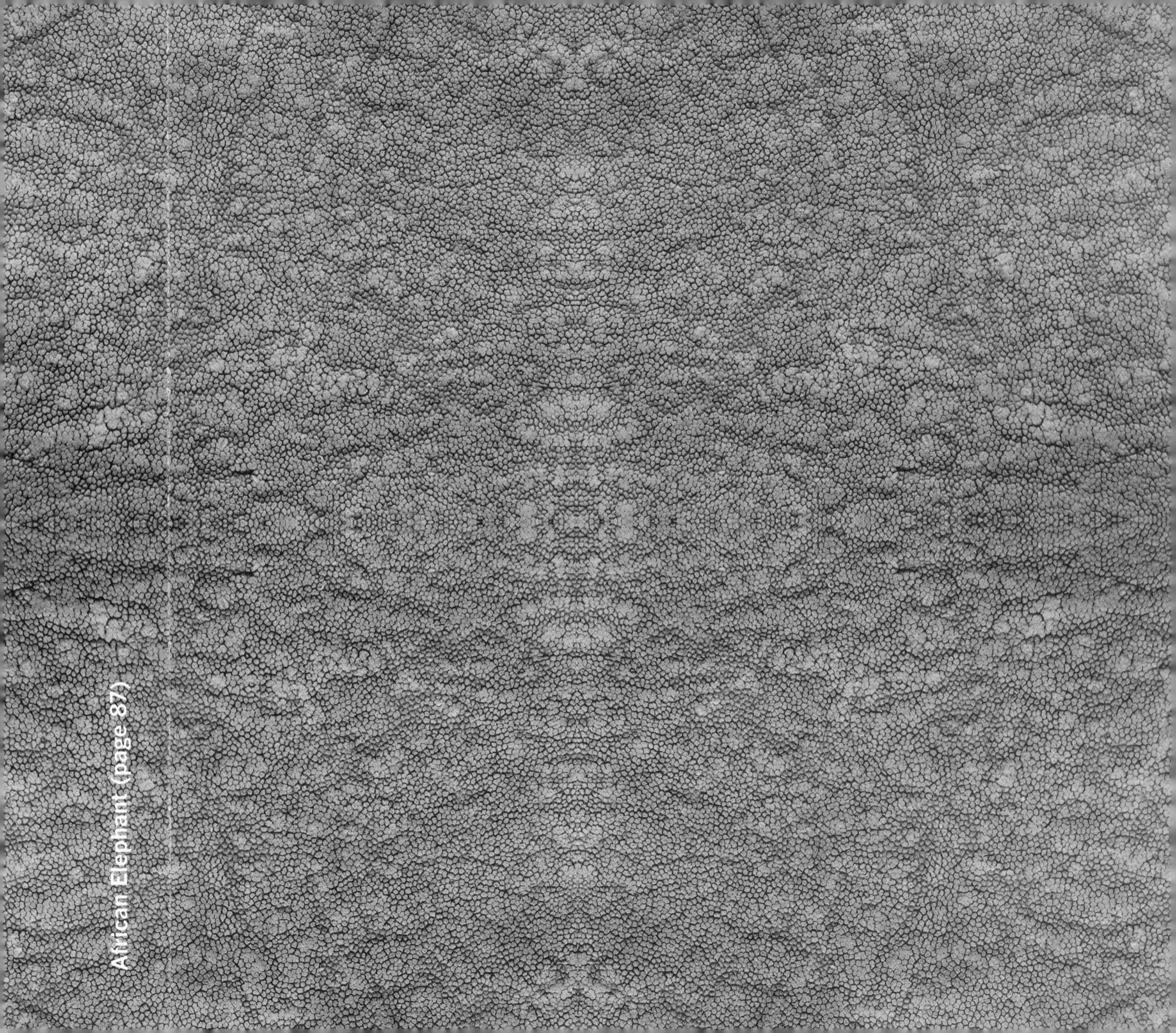

African Elephant (page 87)

African Elephant (page 87)

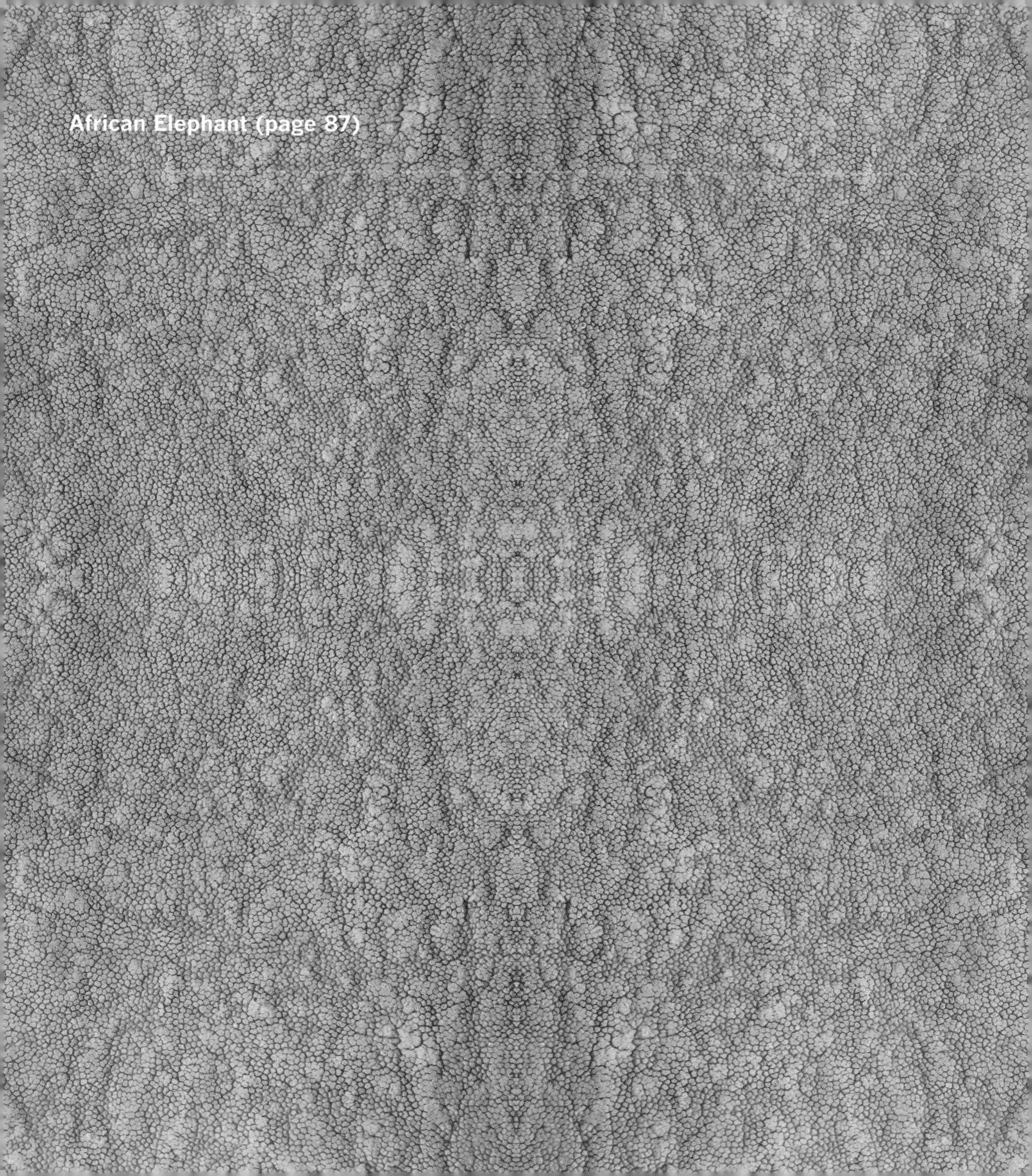

African Elephant (page 87)

African Elephant (page 87)

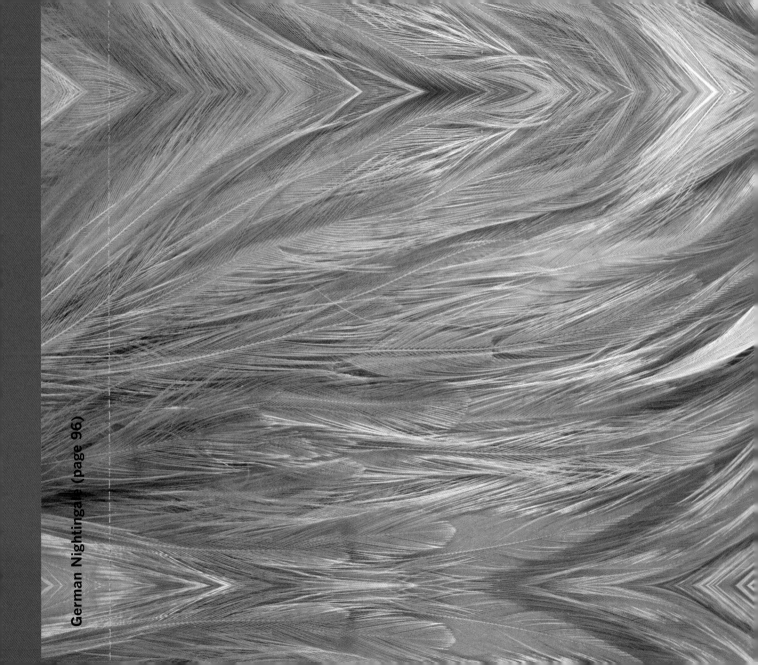

German Nightingale (page 96)

German Nightingale (page 96)

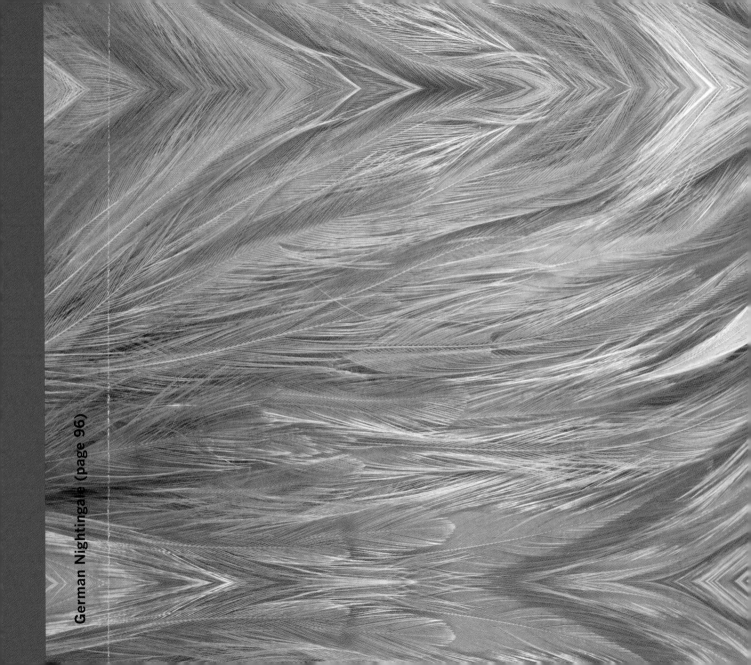

German Nightingale (page 96)

German Nightingale (page 96)

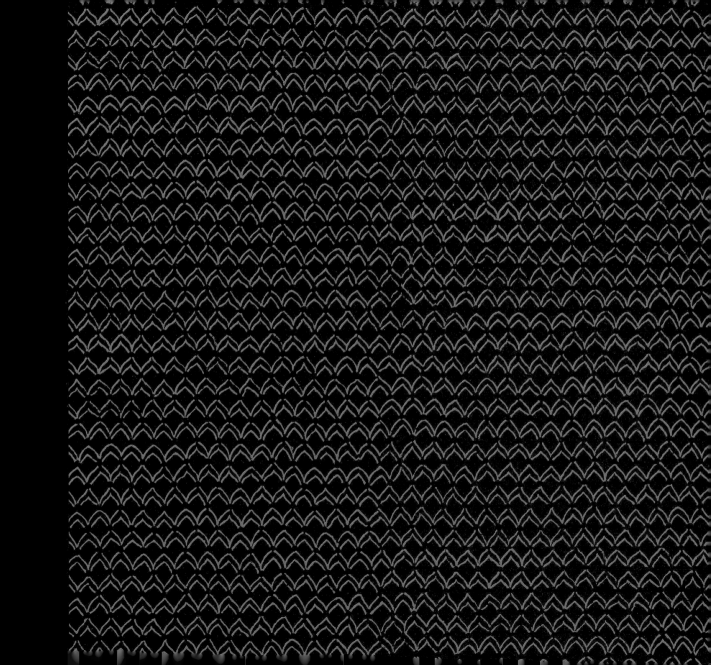

Russian Crow (page 98)

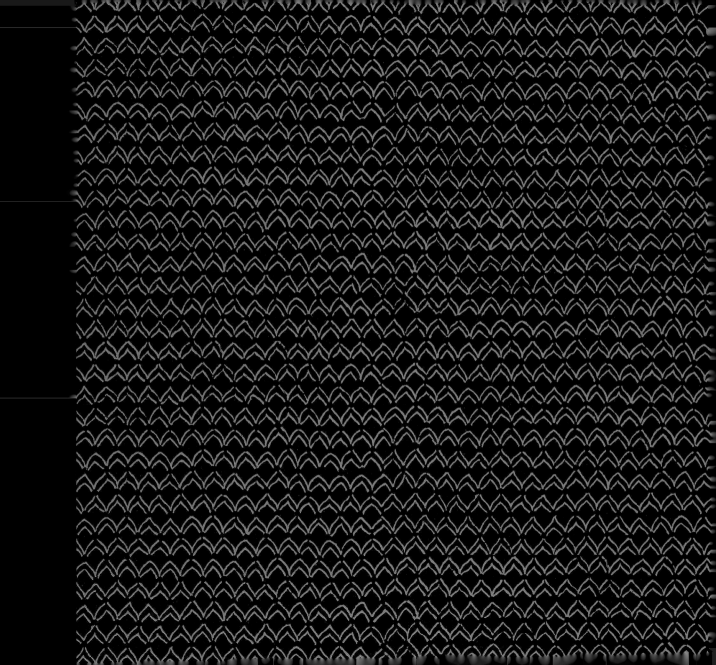

Russian Crow (page 98)

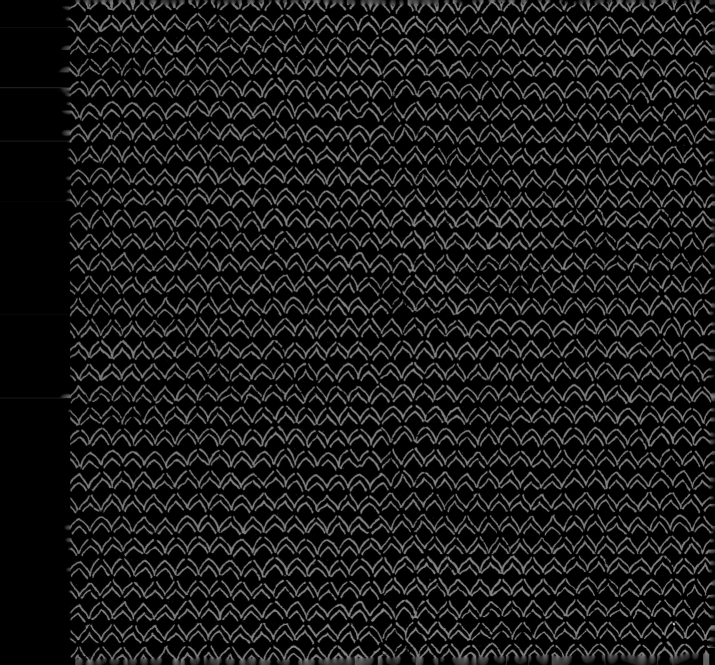

Russian Crow (page 98)

Greek Fish (page 102)

Greek Fish (page 102)

Greek Fish (page 102)

Greek Fish (page 102)

NYC Pigeon (page 105)

NYC Pigeon (page 105)

NYC Pigeon (page 105)

NYC Pigeon (page 105)

Australian Koala Bear (page 108)

Australian Koala Bear (page 108)

Australian Koala Bear (page 108)

Australian Koala Bear (page 108)

Australian Koala Bear (page 108)

Australian Koala Bear (page 108)

Australian Koala Bear (page 108)

Australian Koala Bear (page 108)

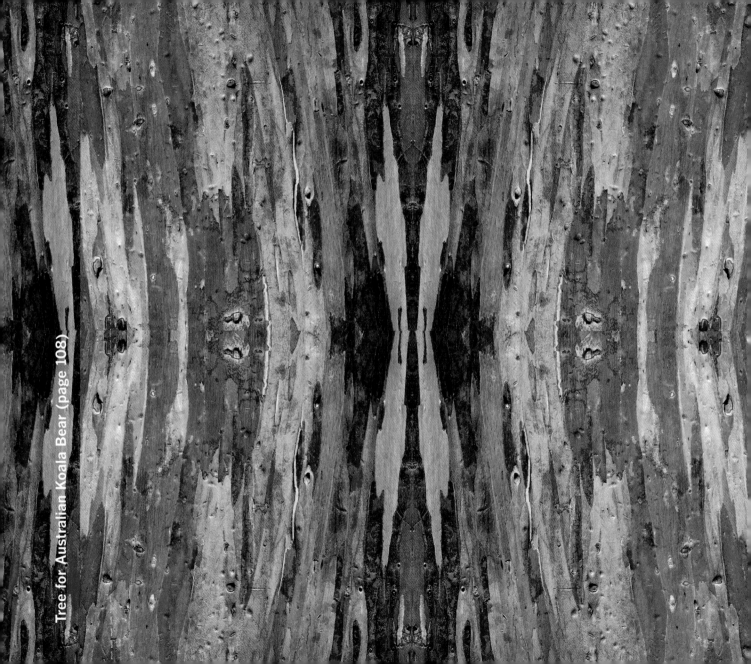

Tree for Australian Koala Bear (page 108)

Tree for Australian Koala Bear Tree (page 108)

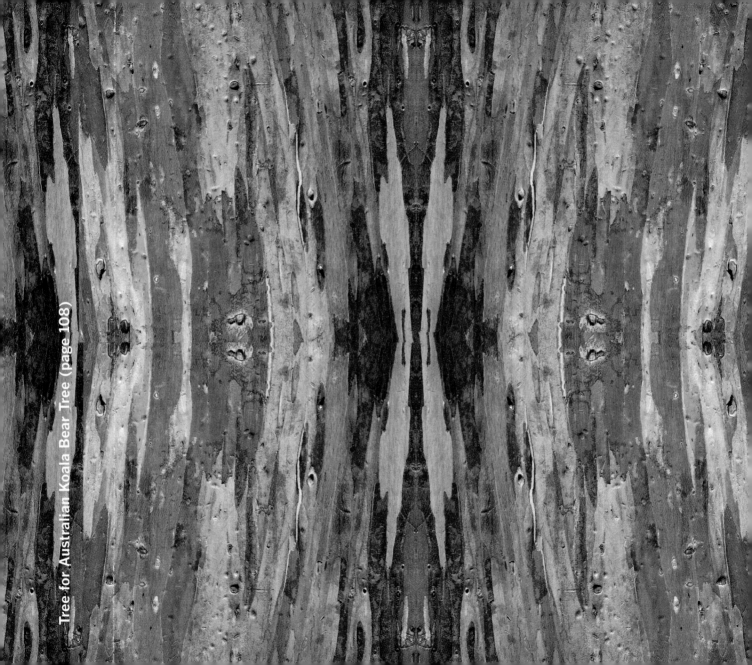

Tree for Australian Koala Bear Tree (page 108)

Tree for Australian Koala Bear Tree (page 108)

Agra Peacock (page 111)

Agra Peacock (page 111)

Agra Peacock (page 111)

Agra Peacock (page 111)

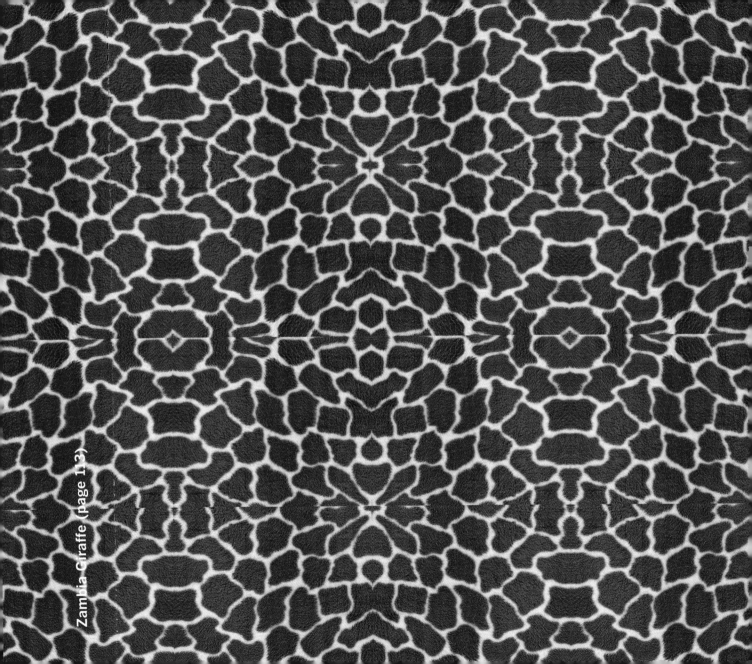

Zambia Giraffe (page 113)

Zambia Giraffe (page 113)

Chinese Opera Hat (page 122)

Chinese Opera Hat (page 122)

Chinese Opera Hat (page 122)

Japanese Samurai Helmet (page 127)

Canadian Canoe (page 130)

Canadian Canoe (page 130)

Canadian Canoe (page 130)

Canadian Canoe (page 130)

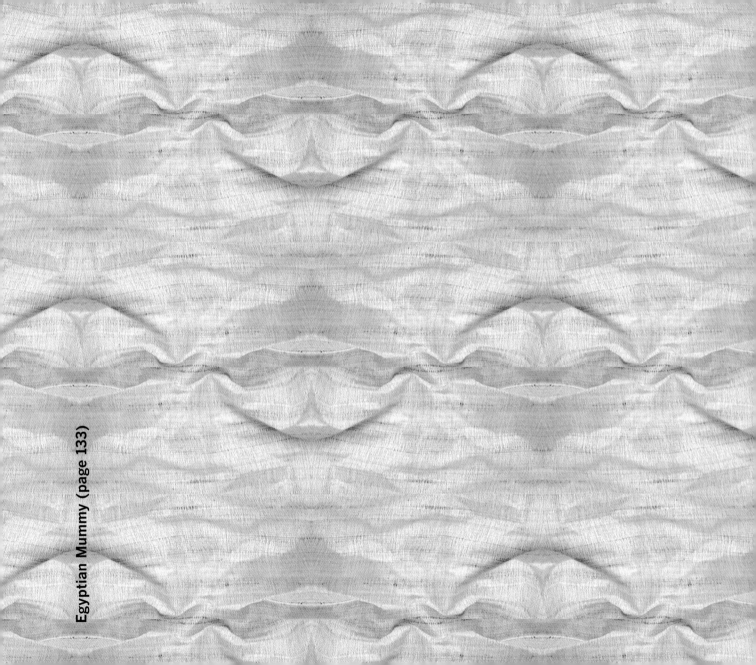

Egyptian Mummy (page 133)

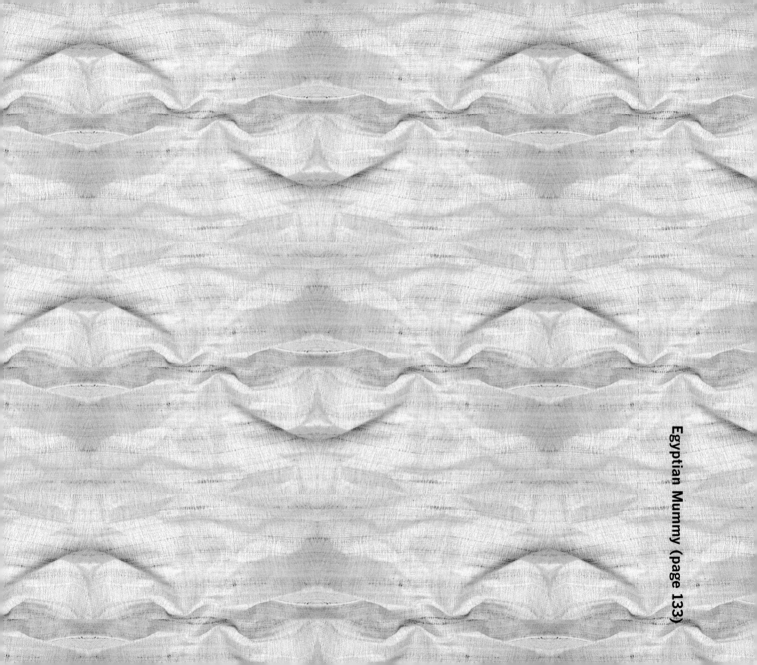

Egyptian Mummy (page 133)

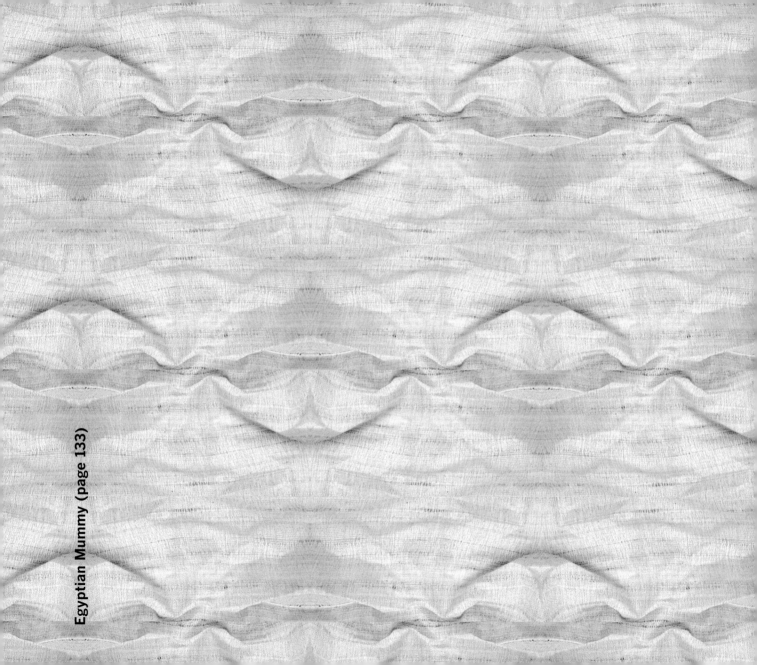

Egyptian Mummy (page 133)

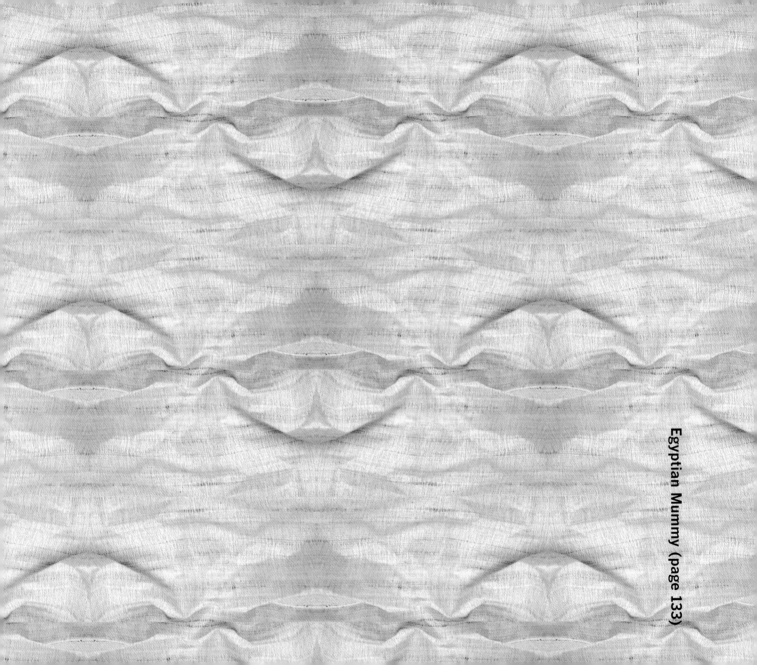

Egyptian Mummy (page 133)

Hollywood Star (page 136)

Hollywood Star (page 136)

Hollywood Star (page 136)

Hollywood Star (page 136)

Hollywood Star (page 136)

Hollywood Star (page 136)

Gift Box (page 142)

Gift Box (page 142)

Gift Box (page 142)